Praise for Marjorie Dannenfelser and *Life Is Winning*

"As an advocate for life at every stage, it is usually my firm decision to avoid politics in a public way. I have great respect for the power of every human right, including the right to vote and the right to live. Marjorie's journey from pro-choice to a life advocate and her tireless passionate work on behalf of children is truly inspiring. One of the many beautiful arcs of *Life Is Winning* is Marjorie's understanding of Merriam Webster's definition of child, which is from conception to adolescence. The reality that millions of children lose their lives because of political stances isn't comprehensible until you read this book. This testament takes a journey which reveals an astounding truth and explains how human rights are lost every day under the artificial shield of women's rights. As a feminist, I will never shame any woman who has had an abortion and as an advocate for life, I will lobby with all my strength for every child to be born, except in those rare instances where birth would endanger the mother's life. *Life Is Winning* removes the thoughts of confusion and brings into sharp focus the clarity of a 'medical procedure' that is haunting and heartbreaking, leaving women scarred emotionally and often physically for the rest of their lives. Whatever your political beliefs, whatever your faith, indeed, if you are an atheist, liberal or conservative, please read *Life Is Winning*. It has the power and strength to change and save lives."

> —Kathy Ireland
> Chair & CEO, Kathy Ireland Worldwide and Life Advocate

"In this book, you will see what courageous leadership looks like as you learn how Marjorie has led the fight for the most basic of all human rights–that the vulnerable and marginalized must be protected. She challenges us to consider a moral choice—will we stand together and recognize the dignity of the unborn? Will we renew our commitment to life and liberty for all people? This is hard work. *Life Is Winning* shows you how it is done."

> —Cheryl Bachelder
> Former CEO, Popeyes Louisiana Kitchen, and
> Author of *Dare to Serve*

"It takes enormous courage and faith to dare to be countercultural, whether in business or politics, when the stakes are high and success by no means guaranteed. That's what I so admire about Marjorie. In *Life Is Winning* she recounts her own change of heart and the enormous challenges she faced as leader of a young organization striving to change the culture in Washington on one of the gravest moral issues of our time—all with the candor, vulnerability, and urgent sense of purpose that has made her and Susan B. Anthony List such an effective model of servant leadership for decades. Highly recommend!"

> —Horst Schulze
> CEO of Horst Schulze Consulting, Co-Founder and
> Former President and COO of Ritz-Carlton Hotels,
> Founder and Former CEO of Capella Hotels

"*Life Is Winning* offers a rich account of the great modern-day civil rights cause that is the pro-life movement. From the earliest efforts in Congress to reverse the devastating fallout of *Roe v. Wade*, to President Trump's stunning victory and extraordinary leadership on life, my friend and Heritage Foundation alumna Marjorie Dannenfelser puts the movement's recent history and current battles in context and presents a vision for the future that veterans of the movement and newcomers alike will find compelling. Her compassion for mothers and babies, tenacity in fighting for justice, and faith in the American people guided by God shine throughout."

> —Kay C. James, President, The Heritage Foundation

"One of the most terrifying, yet empowering things a person can do is to admit, 'I was wrong,' and then take a leap of faith and step across the threshold into an entirely different way of living. As a former Planned Parenthood director, I believed I was helping women—deceiving not only them but also myself. My illusions shattered the day I came face to face with the violent reality of abortion. As a fellow convert to the pro-life cause, Marjorie has traveled the same path as countless Americans whose eyes have been opened and *are* being opened to the plight of unborn children and mothers. I commend Marjorie for having the courage to follow the truth, to share her story and insights in this enlightening book, and most importantly, to act and speak out for those who have no voice. Life is winning because pro-life is pro-love and because every human being has inherent dignity."

> —Abby Johnson
> Pro-life Advocate, Bestselling Author and Speaker;
> CEO and Founder of And Then There Were None Ministry

"Susan B. Anthony List's modern political grassroots fight for unborn children and their mothers consciously invokes that of suffrage movement pioneers, who championed the dignity of all people regardless of race, sex, or physical ability. *Life Is Winning* reveals how Marjorie Dannenfelser grew the Susan B. Anthony List into a powerful force for lobbying and electing pro-life leaders, especially pro-life women. Dannenfelser and SBA List have never backed down from confronting elite politicians about the necessity of prioritizing innocent human life, and their message and strategy have proven effective from the statehouse all the way up to the presidency."

> —Kimberly Cook
> Author and host of *The Dignity of Women Podcast*

"Those of us in the U.S. Senate who have the privilege of standing with President Trump to fight for innocent life could not ask for better allies than Marjorie and Susan B. Anthony List. As Marjorie so persuasively argues, despite growing extremism on the pro-abortion side, the pro-life movement is stronger than ever. This is a battle we must win—and by God's grace and thanks to the tireless work of pro-life advocates across America, we are winning."

> —U.S. Senator Steve Daines (R-MT)
> Founder of the Senate Pro-Life Caucus

"Any time I've interviewed Marjorie, she's been incredibly generous in sharing her pro-life insight and expertise with me and my audience. I shouldn't be surprised that it's in this same generous spirit Marjorie details her personal pro-life journey in *Life Is Winning* for all of us. And it is a journey: before Marjorie became a prominent national pro-life figure, she was the 'pro-choice leader' of Duke University's College Republicans. Marjorie's perspective, therefore, can't help but be shaped by her conversion. In *Life Is Winning*, Marjorie shares many of the life-affirming realities she's experienced: whether it's been in her own family life or on those emotional-roller-coaster election nights. As a reader, it's a privilege to have the curtain pulled back on all the politics of the pro-life movement. There are stories in here that only Marjorie can tell, as she's a true mover-and-shaker for the pro-life cause in Washington, D.C. The pages that fill this book are filled with Marjorie's signature hope: a hope Marjorie holds for others, a hope Marjorie holds for the pro-life movement, and a hope anchored in her faith."

> —Catherine Hadro
> Host, EWTN Pro-Life Weekly

"Marjorie and her team at the Susan B. Anthony List are doing God's work. She knows being pro-life is not about being for or against women. It is about being for a baby's right to live—the most basic right there is. Through honest reflection and personal insight, in *Life Is Winning*, Marjorie shows us not only why she has been a moral leader for decades but why she is one of our country's most savvy political forces."

>—Nikki Haley
>   Former governor of South Carolina, UN Ambassador,
>   and *New York Times* Bestselling Author

"As president of the nation's largest pro-life youth organization, I can attest that Marjorie's new book absolutely nails the state of the pro-life movement in 2020. As she has highlighted, the success and momentum of this cause is driven in large part by my generation's increasingly pro-life views—contrary to what the abortion lobby and their friends in politics, Hollywood, and the media would have us all believe. *Life Is Winning* is essential reading, not only for my generation to see the powerful impact of their voices, but for all who wish to understand why pro-life advocates are more fired up than ever to win in 2020 and ultimately to end abortion in our time."

>—Kristan Hawkins
>   President, Students for Life of America

"*Life Is Winning* provides a key to making sense of the pro-abortion Left's endless campaign to remove President Trump and the vitriol directed at Justice Brett Kavanaugh. Political events like these are virtually inexplicable without reference to *Roe v. Wade's* noxious influence and faulty foundations. Susan B. Anthony List's unique focus on winning the political battle to restore protection of human life in the law has renewed the pro-life movement's hope of victory—not in some remote future, but with each election and every pro-life ballot cast, especially in this crucial year."

>—Mollie Hemingway
>   Bestselling Author of *Justice on Trial*

"The story of how Marjorie Dannenfelser and the SBA List became a political and pro-life powerhouse, setting the stage for the Trump/Pence victory, is the key to understanding the outcome of the 2016 election."

—Deal W. Hudson
    President, Morley Institute Church and Culture &
    Author of *Onward Christian Soldiers: The Growing Political
    Power of Catholics and Evangelicals in the United States*

"Marjorie excellently portrays the position of the pro-life movement throughout this book. Her inspiring conversion story has touched many, and as a longtime friend, I have been blessed to fight alongside her in the battle to save unborn children. Now is the time for Americans to mobilize and speak up. We must engage together, as a unified movement, to end the greatest injustice of our time: the killing of countless innocent babies and wounding of their mothers. We will never stop fighting until this vital mission is accomplished."

—Penny Young Nance
    CEO and President, Concerned Women for America

"If you want to understand why we have the most pro-life president in our history, and how a strong pro-life movement can elect him again, read *Life Is Winning*. You'll understand how the pro-life message wins elections, and will be inspired with lessons from a woman with whom I've been privileged to collaborate for decades!"

—Fr. Frank Pavone
    National Director, Priests for Life and Co-Chair,
    Pro-life Voices for Trump

"At the heart of *Life Is Winning* is the idea of transformation—Marjorie's search for truth that led her to be one of the nation's strongest advocates for the sanctity of human life, President Trump's journey to becoming one of history's greatest pro-life champions, and of America as nation rejecting Court imposed abortion on demand as a defining characteristic of our country. It is a story of turning back toward fundamental truth, and our nation's founding principles told with compassion and keen insight by a pro-life trailblazer in her own right."

—Tony Perkins
    President, Family Research Council

"Marjorie has spent decades fiercely devoted to empowering the pro-life grassroots and promoting courageous leaders in elected office who will fight for legal protections for our preborn brothers and sisters. Our movement is strengthened by her and SBA List's tireless advocacy, which are essential today in our shared fight to restore the right to life for every child."

—Lila Rose

"A deeply perceptive analysis of the political and cultural forces that propelled President Trump to victory, to the surprise and chagrin not only of pro-abortion elites, but also a consultant class that wrote off the 'social issues' . . . four years later, as President Trump delivers on his promises, the same deeply-held pro-life, pro-family, and pro-freedom values that turned out millions of Americans to the polls to elect him continue to motivate his most passionate supporters. I appreciate Marjorie and SBA List for their dedication to championing pro-life causes and ensuring we protect the most vulnerable."

—Mercedes Schlapp
    Senior Advisor for Strategic Communications,
    Donald J. Trump for President

"Life is the most basic of all our liberties. It is not negotiable. If we don't stand up for this most important of all liberties, especially the innocent in the womb and on the day of birth, then all other professions of defending freedom are hypocrisy. We have to draw a line in the sand and not compromise on this issue. That's why I love Marjorie Dannenfelser and the work being done through Susan B. Anthony List. Marjorie is relentless and well qualified to lead this fight. It's my pleasure to endorse her new book and just as the title says, 'Life Is Winning.' We are on the verge of overturning the scourge of abortion in this land, but the battle isn't won yet. We need Marjorie and SBA List, and you need this book. It will inspire, bless, and equip you to do your part."

—Andrew Wommack
    Founder & President of Andrew Wommack Ministries
    and Charis Bible College

Life Is Winning

Inside the Fight for Unborn Children and Their Mothers

Marjorie Dannenfelser (signature)

MARJORIE DANNENFELSER

Humanix Books

www.humanixbooks.com

Life Is Winning
Humanix Books

Copyright © 2020 by Humanix Books
All rights reserved

Humanix Books, P.O. Box 20989, West Palm Beach, FL 33416, USA
www.humanixbooks.com | info@humanixbooks.com

Library of Congress Cataloguing-in-Publication data is available upon request.

Humanix Books is a division of Humanix Publishing, LLC. Its trademark, consisting of the words "Humanix Books," is registered in the Patent and Trademark Office and in other countries.

ISBN: 978-1-63006-149-4 (Hardcover)
ISBN: 978-1-63006-150-0 (E-book)

Printed in the United States of America
10 9 8 7 6 5 4 3 2 1

Contents

THIS BOOK IS DEDICATED to the memory of the leaders of every successful human rights battle in American history who clung to the promises of our founding documents and pressed to realize them in our laws. At every level of leadership, they worked with love, strategic acumen, determination and righteous impatience to expand the circle of protection for the powerless—each one of whom was first loved by their Creator, then sent to this world with vital and unique purpose. These leaders rejected the utilitarian arguments of the cynics—that somehow liberty was undesirable for the victim and unpleasant for the rest of us.

I also dedicate this book to those who are living this beautiful legacy in the movement to end violence toward the vulnerable before they are born—those fighting against the taking of life and rights at the earliest stage. These modern pro-life leaders, with whom I work every day at Susan B. Anthony List, Charlotte Lozier Institute and in every battleground, understand that the change of heart and mind that shapes our commitment to service to women and children must also change our laws. Great political strategy began with the successful leaders of the past, who made the morally right thing to do the politically smart thing to do by appealing to the better natures and political might of a vast movement. That legacy animates the pro-life movement and is why it will prevail.

Foreword

Sarah Huckabee Sanders

THE TEST OF ANY civilization is how it treats the least among us, and defending life is what makes America special. The pro-life movement in America has persisted in the face of adversity for nearly half a century, but I truly believe it has never been stronger than right now—and *Life Is Winning* makes that case in a compelling and winsome way.

Strong pro-life values run in my family. It is this issue that prompted my father to run for U.S. Senate. Along the way there have always been naysayers who would discourage candidates from bringing up the subject of abortion, for fear of losing elections. Since 1993 the naysayers have more than met their match in Susan B. Anthony List and its heroic leader Marjorie Dannenfelser. *Life Is Winning* proves that we don't have to compromise our pro-life principles or stay silent about the things that matter most.

I admire Marjorie's courage in forging a totally new path, and her story reminds me of my own experience. When other kids were on summer vacation, I was working on my dad's campaign. He didn't have staff—we were it. We stuffed envelopes, put up signs, and went door to door. Likewise, SBA List didn't have the money of the abortion lobby, or prestige, or institutional support. What they had was a righteous cause, savvy strategy, and the grit and determination to see it through—and they have laid crucial groundwork for pro-life women and men to thrive in politics.

There is no substitute for meeting voters face to face, where they are. That old-school shoe leather work, combined with unrivaled passion for the life issue, wins elections and makes SBA List unique among pro-life organizations. And it was instrumental in electing my former boss, President Donald Trump, the most pro-life president in history.

I'm beyond proud of all we have accomplished together with President Trump in the White House. It was the greatest honor and adventure to go to work every day serving in the administration of a true patriot who knows that for America to be great, we must stand up for the equal value of each human being. One of our proudest moments was when he became the first president to attend the March for Life. Our nation sorely needs leaders who will stand up unabashedly and say, "Every human soul, born and unborn, is made in the holy image of God."

America is standing for life again, much to the resentment of powerful elites who want to impose their radical abortion agenda by fiat. Ever since this president took office they have been fighting to undermine and override the will of the people. They slandered and tried to destroy Justice Kavanaugh, and they attempted to impeach President Trump and remove him from office.

But in spite of the extremism of pro-abortion Democrats and the constant negativity of the media, President Trump's adversaries have succeeded in doing one thing: uniting the Republican Party like never before—especially in fighting to protect the value and dignity of every human life. And it couldn't have happened without Marjorie and SBA List. Thanks to their efforts, competing to be the biggest champion for unborn children and their mothers is the new standard for both the presidency and the Republican Party.

While it was a great privilege to serve in the Trump administration, my most important job is being a mom to my three kids. Being the first mother to hold the position of White House Press Secretary was one of the most challenging experiences of my life, but also incredibly rewarding. It is so important that women and mothers be able to see themselves active and succeeding in politics—to envision bringing all their talent and creativity to bear to change our policies and make our country a better place, just as Susan B. Anthony and her contemporaries did and just as their modern heirs in the pro-life movement do today. It makes no sense that in the most prosperous and free country in the history of the world, anyone would still be telling women they have to choose between their dreams and their children—but that's precisely what the abortion movement does. When we reject this demeaning double standard, life wins.

It's been said that all that is necessary for evil to triumph is for good men to do nothing.

For almost thirty years, the grassroots activists of SBA List have stood in the gap and fought for what is right. Their tireless efforts have brought us to the cusp of victory and shown the way to engage—but each of us has a role to play. There has never been a more urgent moment for each and every American who cares about life to stand up.

Introduction

Vice President Mike Pence

MORE THAN **240** YEARS ago, our founders wrote words that have echoed throughout the ages. They declared "these Truths to be self-evident," that we are, each of us, endowed by our "Creator with certain unalienable Rights, [and] that among these are Life, Liberty, and the Pursuit of Happiness."

Forty-seven years ago, the Supreme Court of the United States turned its back on the unalienable right to life. But in that moment, a movement began—a movement that continues to win hearts and minds; a movement defined by generosity, compassion, and love; and a movement that today, with President Donald Trump leading the charge, is energized and unified as never before.

From preventing taxpayer dollars from funding abortion overseas, to empowering states to defund abortion providers and Title X, to nominating judges who will uphold our God-given liberties enshrined in the Constitution of the United States, President Trump has been a tireless defender of life and conscience in America.

Today, thanks to the leadership of President Trump and the compassion, persistence, and prayer of the pro-life movement, life is winning in America.

Life is winning in a new generation of pro-life leaders who have stepped forward from the White House to statehouses across the country. Life is winning through the generosity of millions of adoptive families who open their hearts and homes to children in need. Life is winning through the compassion of caregivers and volunteers at pro-life pregnancy centers and faith-based organizations who minister to women in cities and towns across America. And life is winning through the steady advance of science that illuminates daily the humanity of the unborn child and the truth about when life begins.

Life is winning through the quiet counsel between mothers and daughters, grandmothers and granddaughters, between friends across kitchen tables and over coffee on college campuses. The truth about abortion is being told. Compassion is overcoming convenience, and hope is defeating despair.

The battle to restore the right to life has been long and hard fought—and for many years now, my friend Marjorie Dannenfelser has been at the vanguard, bringing both wise counsel and principled leadership to the cause. As president of the Susan B. Anthony List, she has led an impressive effort over the last three elections to reach more than 4.6 million voters and elect a pro-life president and a pro-life majority in the United States Senate.

In these pages, Marjorie has precisely captured how far the pro-life movement has come and how much we stand to achieve at this pivotal moment. It has never been more critical for each of us to continue to stand up and speak out. As Thomas Jefferson once wrote, "God who gave us life gave us liberty. Can the liberties of a nation be secure when we have removed a conviction that these liberties are the gift of God?"

This moment calls for every ounce of our energy and enthusiasm. It requires our full determination and conviction, our passion, and our prayers. It will be the ultimate test of the character and faith at the heart of this movement. But I trust that this important book will encourage and inspire the government to play an even greater role in restoring the sanctity of life to the center of American law and to encourage us never to doubt that the Author of Life is with us in these efforts. *Life Is Winning.*

Preface

As this book was being prepared for publication, and as Susan B. Anthony List was about to expand our ground efforts in 2020 battleground states, the entire world was rocked by the coronavirus pandemic. In a matter of weeks, this unforeseen crisis altered daily life nationwide, caused SBA List to adapt our operations dramatically, and could permanently change the way Americans vote.

It has also made each of us reflect on what is essential. Americans fundamentally value life. Were it not so, the heroic sacrifices made by millions of our neighbors would be inconceivable. The way our country has united to save the vulnerable has drawn comparisons to the Greatest Generation when faced with the existential threat of World War II. In times of crisis, our instincts run to those living in the shadows, those who could most easily slip through the cracks.

The abortion lobby has been a notable exception, preying on fear and sacrificing women's health and children's lives—not to mention public health and their own employees' safety—all for profit. While cancer treatments and countless other "elective" procedures were being postponed, abortion businesses like Planned Parenthood have insisted on keeping their doors open at taxpayer expense, diverting precious resources from the front lines. Even worse, the abortion industry and their allies in the media and the Democratic Party have pushed to expand the use of dangerous abortion drugs via telemedicine and the mail.

In his presidential campaign, Joe Biden has sealed the Democratic Party's capitulation to extremism, declaring abortion "essential health care that cannot be delayed" even during a national emergency. Meanwhile abortion extremists finally succeeded in expelling a pro-life hero, Illinois Democrat Dan Lipinski, from Congress after fifteen years.

Anyone who has witnessed the Democratic Party's decades-long, radical shift on abortion knows how far the party has strayed from its roots—but the story of the abortion movement in America is one of slow decline. Indeed, from *Roe v. Wade* on they have steadily lost the American people, while the pro-life movement's youthfulness, energy, and momentum have increased.

From the rise of EMILY's List in the early 1990s, to the movement's pinnacle in the Obama years, the abortion lobby scored wins politically and in the courts but failed to heed warnings about their political saliency and the weakness of their moral infrastructure—such as former NARAL president Nancy Keenan's exclamation upon seeing the 2010 March for Life crowd: *"There are so many of them, and they are so young."*

Within the Republican Party, the life issue has gone from liability to asset. In contrast to the Democrats, today "Republican" is virtually synonymous with "pro-life." President Trump and a majority of the Senate along with GOP governors proudly and publicly embrace the pro-life movement. All this became possible because we exercised our political muscle and never gave up—a largely untold story, until now.

Biden's career spans the same arc of time. Whether opportunistic or sincere, his conversion to the extreme proabortion position runs counter to America's conversion. In doubling down, he is gambling that it will work to his advantage, in spite of enormous and mounting evidence to the contrary. He is likely America's last thoroughly proabortion presidential candidate.

This a defining moment for our nation. I've often said clarity is a gift in politics, and now the choices and stakes do not get any clearer. As America holds the most consequential election yet for the pro-life cause amid the tumult of a pandemic, the message that life is winning is more timely and necessary than ever.

CHAPTER 1

The Beginnings of Conversion

I AM A CONVERT. THERE was a time when I believed abortion was a good and moral choice. I argued that *Roe v. Wade* was the linchpin of women's rights. I came dangerously close to choosing abortion for myself.

One of the benefits of being a convert is that I recognize the phenomenon in others. I have had the privilege of meeting thousands of pro-life converts. Some have been women who regret their own abortion. Many have been men who are profoundly ashamed of their failure to support both mother and child.

My conversion was akin to what writer Madeleine L'Engle described as "an intellectual acceptance of what my intuition had always known." Some people, however, experience a moment of clarity or a sudden encounter with the truth. Whatever the mechanism, the process of conversion indelibly transforms one's life. The Old Testament prophet Isaiah captures it perfectly: "Remember not the events of the past, the things of long ago consider not; See, I am doing something new! Now it springs forth, do you not perceive it?" (Isaiah 43: 18–19 New American Bible Revised Edition).

When I helped start Susan B. Anthony List (SBA List) more than twenty-five years ago, I hoped and prayed that our nation would experience a conversion that would restore the inalienable right to life for all. The pro-life movement, rooted in the deep soil of the American founding and the character of the American people, has tenaciously worked to restore legal protection for the unborn and has borne much fruit. I never imagined, though, the role that would be played by a playboy real estate tycoon from New York City who was in the news the year of SBA List's launch for divorcing his wife and marrying his mistress, who two months before the wedding had given birth to his child.

Nancy Pelosi once said, "Nothing surprises me. One thing I don't have in my world is surprise." She must have been the only one, then, who was not surprised when Donald J. Trump turned out to be the most pro-life president in American history. I wonder what she was thinking when, as Speaker of the House, she sat behind him during the State of the Union address on February 5, 2019, and heard him say,

> There could be no greater contrast to the beautiful image of a mother holding her infant child than the chilling displays our Nation saw in recent days. Lawmakers in New York cheered with delight upon the passage of legislation that would allow a baby to be ripped from the mother's womb moments before birth. These are living, feeling, beautiful babies who will never get the chance to share their love and dreams with the world. And then we had the case of

the Governor of Virginia, where he basically stated he would execute a baby after birth.

To defend the dignity of every person, I am asking the Congress to pass legislation to prohibit the late-term abortion of children who can feel pain in the mother's womb.

Let us work together to build a culture that cherishes innocent life. And let us reaffirm a fundamental truth: all children—born and unborn—are made in the holy image of God.

I hope when she heard those words, a spirit of conversion started to kindle in her heart as well.

I was with President Trump outside the Oval Office the night before he gave that speech. A small group of leaders of outside policy groups, along with Vice President Mike Pence, Chief of Staff Mick Mulvaney, and presidential advisors Kellyanne Conway and Mercedes Schlapp, had convened to hear a preview of the speech's main themes. The first issue President Trump brought up when he entered the room was the statement Virginia governor Ralph Northam had made a few days earlier in defense of an extreme proabortion bill that had narrowly been defeated in Virginia's legislature. The bill's sponsor, Delegate Kathy Tran, had made clear that her bill permitted abortion through all nine months of pregnancy, even as the woman is "about to give birth." Asked by the media what this would mean if a full-term baby survived an abortion attempt, Governor Northam, a pediatrician, said that the baby would be "resuscitated if that's what the mother and family desired," and the baby would be "kept comfortable" while doctors and parents conferred about whether to provide the care necessary to keep the vulnerable baby alive.

Northam's statement provided an alarming level of clarity about the true intentions of the abortion movement—unlimited abortion on demand, up to the moment of birth and even beyond—a position at odds with the views of the vast majority of Americans. Polls consistently show that only a small minority of Americans support abortion beyond the first trimester of pregnancy. President Trump, a gifted politician as well as a convert, knows a wedge issue when he sees one. The line about Governor Northam was added to the speech on the spot and continues to be a huge applause line at Trump rallies.

Lawmakers in Virginia, New York, and other states were pushed to take such an extreme stance on abortion by an abortion lobby that fears, with good reason, that *Roe v. Wade*'s days are numbered. That fear was on full display during the confirmation of Brett Kavanaugh to the Supreme Court. Kavanaugh was Trump's second appointment to the high court and the first that could tip the balance against *Roe*.

Trump's first appointment was of Neil Gorsuch to take the place of Justice Antonin Scalia, whose unexpected death in February 2016 had in part laid the groundwork for Trump's victory. Exit polling on Election Day revealed that the future composition of the Supreme Court was the top issue for 21 percent of all voters—and they preferred Trump to Hillary Clinton by a margin of 56 to 41 percent. Eleven days after his inauguration, President Trump delivered on his promise to appoint a justice "in the mold" of Scalia, a brilliant jurist who, according to legal scholar Edward Whelan, "vigorously exposed the lie, first propagated in *Roe v. Wade* and then perpetuated in *Planned Parenthood v. Casey*, that the Constitution somehow denies American citizens the authority to protect the lives of unborn human beings."

SBA List mobilized all our resources to support Gorsuch's nomination, and the proabortion forces did the same in opposition. But given that his confirmation would not fundamentally change the balance of the court, the effort on both sides felt a bit like Captain Louis Renault in *Casablanca* rounding up the usual suspects. A Justice Gorsuch was necessary to overturning *Roe* but not sufficient.

Justice Kavanaugh, on the other hand, may be sufficient.

Justice Anthony Kennedy's decision to resign in June 2018 and allow President Trump to appoint a successor decisively shifted the momentum on the abortion issue in favor of the right to life. The abortion lobby knew it immediately and reacted with a fury unlike anything I have ever witnessed. The target of that fury was Trump's nominee, Brett Kavanaugh.

Because of SBA List's efforts on behalf of Justice Gorsuch's confirmation, we were privy to some of the discussions that led to Kavanaugh's selection. I was happy with the choice. Kavanaugh was known as an originalist jurist, and he had a strong record of protecting life and constitutional rights. I was at the White House for the announcement and pledged that SBA List would mobilize the pro-life grassroots nationwide and in key Senate battleground states. I knew that given what was at stake in the confirmation process, it would be much more difficult than Gorsuch's. I knew we could take nothing for granted. But I also knew that there was a pro-life majority in the Senate—one we had worked hard to elect—and I believed that ultimately Kavanaugh would easily have the votes to be confirmed. Boy, was I wrong about the easy part.

Maybe I should have taken a page from Nancy Pelosi's book and not been surprised, but I was taken aback by the extremes to which the opposition would go to smear Justice Kavanaugh. The last-minute emergence of a woman accusing Kavanaugh of teenage sexual misconduct—accusations that Kavanaugh unequivocally denied and for which there was not one shred of corroborating evidence—was handled in a duplicitous and reckless way. But it also laid bare a crucial and encouraging fact: the citadel of *Roe v. Wade* had been breached, the walls were crumbling, and its defenders were under siege.

I was invited to sit in the Senate Judiciary hearing room on the days when Judge Kavanaugh and his accuser testified. It was a surreal experience. I sat down next to a woman I had never seen before. Watching from our offices in Northern Virginia, SBA List's communications director, Mallory Quigley, texted me to say the woman was actress/activist Alyssa Milano, a vocal abortion advocate and a leader of the #MeToo movement against sexual assault. It is easy to demonize from afar; it's much more difficult face-to-face. Despite being on opposite sides of the issue at hand—and many others—our interactions were marked by mutual kindness. I profoundly opposed her efforts and those with whom she was allied to unjustly accuse Brett Kavanaugh in an effort to defeat his nomination. But at the end of the day, we took each other's hands, and I said, "I know we don't see eye to eye on some things, but I want you to know how deeply I admire what you've done to help women who have been abused." She replied, "I appreciate that so much. Makes me a little weepy."

The #MeToo movement and the proabortion movement had merged, and little wonder. Women are the first victims of abortion, an outcome too often forced on them by predatory men who have sought pleasure without any concern for the consequences. The Kavanaugh nomination had become a proxy for all that pain; defeating Kavanaugh was to them defeating every man that had hurt them or their friends or might one day hurt their daughters. I hope that one day they will see that it is abortion itself that opened wide the door for the use and abuse of women without constraint by predators who care nothing for their well-being. The founders of the feminist movement knew this—that's why they so vigorously opposed and denounced abortion. I believe that a refounding of that movement in a post-*Roe* world will embrace this truth again.

I admired President Trump's willingness to stand by his nominee despite the media and political frenzy and the hand-wringing of some weak-kneed members of his party in the Senate (looking at you, former senator Jeff Flake). But still I worried a little after the bruising battle to confirm Justice Kavanaugh that President Trump might become wary about engaging in the pro-life battle. Instead, it has emboldened him. The president's comments on life in the State of the Union were the most explicit made on the issue by any president in that address. Shortly thereafter, the White House asked SBA List to coordinate a group of people to meet with the president to underscore his commitment to signing the Pain-Capable Unborn Child Protection Act, a legislation to ban abortion after five months of pregnancy, at a point at least by which unborn babies can feel pain.

The date the White House chose was February 14—Valentine's Day—the perfect date to celebrate the love that propels and sustains the pro-life movement. Among the people there were Micah Pickering and his parents, Clayton and Danielle. Micah was born after just twenty-two weeks in the womb. Doctors told Micah's parents he would suffer from severe disabilities and asked if they should resuscitate him upon birth. Clayton and Danielle said yes without hesitation. Today Micah is a perfectly healthy eight-year-old boy. He has become the face of the

Pain-Capable Unborn Child Protection Act, which has been nicknamed "Micah's Law."

Also present was Melissa Ohden, who survived a late-term abortion and was given medical care by nurses over the objections of some medical personnel; today she is the mother of two and the nation's leading advocate for infants born alive after abortions. Christina Marie Bennett, whose mother walked out moments before aborting her after a hospital janitor encouraged her to have her baby, was there, as was Katie Shaw, an adult with Down syndrome whose parents made the increasingly rare choice not to abort her. Katie offered key testimony in support of a law protecting children with disabilities from abortion that was signed into law in Indiana by then governor Mike Pence.

Most of the guests were meeting the president for the first time, but one—five-year-old Katharine Alexander—was renewing her acquaintance with an old friend. Katharine first met President Trump a year earlier, at SBA List's annual gala. At that event, the president told Katharine's story to a hushed crowd of more than one thousand people gathered at the Washington, DC, National Building Museum.

He said,

This organization bears the name of one of the greatest champions of freedom in American history: Susan B. Anthony. She fought for decades to end slavery, to secure women's right to vote, and to respect the dignity of every single person. A great person, a great woman, was she.

Now we have a chance to honor her legacy and restore the first right in the Declaration of Independence. It's called the right to life. Here with us this evening are Lisa and Bruce Alexander, and their family, from Gaithersburg, Maryland. Good place. In January of 2012, the Alexanders attended the March for Life, and God put it in their hearts to adopt a beautiful child. Two years later, in January of 2014, the Alexanders got a call that a baby had been born, who was opioid-dependent. She desperately needed a loving home. She was in serious, serious trouble. And the Alexanders welcomed her into their home with wide-open arms.

After the baby was treated for opioid withdrawal, they brought home their new and very beautiful daughter, Katharine. Hi, Katharine. Hi. Come on up here, Katharine. Come on. Katharine is four years old, and she is full of incredible energy, spirit, and talent. At the age of two—come on up, Katharine—she memorized "America the Beautiful." She recites poetry. And recently she announced to her dad that when she grows up she wants to be a famous police officer. And then, when she gets tired of that, she wants to become President. That's okay with her. She'll be President someday.

Every time Katharine's older siblings come home from school, Katharine runs into their arms and gives them a great, big, beautiful hug. They're amazed by how much she loves them and how much they love her.

So tonight, we celebrate you, Katharine. We celebrate your life. Thank you, darling.

I knew the president was going to talk about Katharine and her parents in his speech that night, but I never thought he would invite her up on stage. What an incredible moment that was. The president showed to the whole world watching that evening via the news media who and what the pro-life movement is all about—the precious child, the loving family, the hope for the future.

Katharine—about to be reunited with her friend the president—bounced into the room when the Oval Office doors opened. With me in introducing the other guests were Dr. Alveda King, one of the most effective pro-life spokeswomen in the world, who seamlessly connects the civil rights struggle led by her uncle, Dr. Martin Luther King Jr., to the battle to protect the unborn, and the president's friend and advisor Pastor Paula White. President Trump then gave remarks to a group of thousands of people assembled on a conference call in which he introduced the group with him in the room, called attention to the extremism of today's Democrats, and reiterated his pledge to fight for the unborn, especially babies who survive failed abortions.

After the call, the president had an intimate conversation with the group and heard their stories. He listens well. At the end of the conversation, the president specifically wanted a picture with the children—Katharine Alexander and Micah Pickering. Katharine immediately ran up behind the desk with the president. The president, broadly smiling, looked at us and said with a wink, "I'm not going to compete with her!"

CHAPTER 2

Donald Trump Closes the Gap

AFTER NEARLY EIGHT YEARS of the Obama administration, which did everything in its power to expand abortion on demand and provide taxpayer funding for it at home and abroad, our SBA List team was highly energized to elect a president in 2016 who would reverse Obama's policies and support laws and appoint judges who would defend and uphold the right to life. We began preparing for the 2016 presidential election before the November 2014 midterms. By early 2015, when many presidential hopefuls had already formed exploratory committees, we asked all the candidates to make two simple commitments: to sign the Pain-Capable Unborn Child Protection Act and to strip Planned Parenthood, the nation's largest abortion business, of the more than half a billion dollars in taxpayer funds it receives each year. The legislative groundwork was laid for both of those priorities—the House had passed a bill to defund Planned Parenthood several times and was set to vote on the Pain-Capable bill. One decisive obstacle stood in the way: the veto pen of President Barack Obama. The 2016 election was our opportunity to elect a president who would sign these pro-life priorities into law.

By the spring of 2015, the potential presidential field in the Republican primary was beginning to get crowded—it would eventually grow to seventeen. Almost every candidate had a proven pro-life record to run on. Jeb Bush was the early frontrunner, with an enormous war chest and a successful record as governor of Florida, a must-win state for Republicans. Although we did not personally meet until after the campaign, we spoke at length on the phone one sweltering summer day in 2014 while I sat in my car in front of my favorite bakery in Arlington, Virginia. He wanted to talk about an article by *New York Times* reporter Jeremy Peters detailing SBA List's efforts to educate candidates and activists on how to communicate effectively about abortion. Bush's pro-life record as governor was innovative. We talked about the importance of going on offense to expose the extremism of abortion advocates and the wisdom of pursuing legislation to ban abortion after the unborn child feels pain. The spokeswoman for EMILY's List, the largest proabortion political organization in the nation, said, "When it comes to restricting access to abortion, Jeb Bush is as far to the right as you can go." I didn't need any input from the abortion lobby to know that Jeb Bush was a sincere and savvy pro-lifer. I hung up thinking it would be easy to vote for Jeb Bush. Soon after, he endorsed the Pain-Capable Unborn Child Protection Act and pledged to defund Planned Parenthood should he become president. For him, it was a natural fit. He was a true believer.

Bush's rival and fellow Floridian, Senator Marco Rubio, was the favorite candidate of many grassroots activists.

Rubio electrified the crowd at the SBA List gala in 2012 when he said, "There's nothing that America can give this world right now more important than to show that all life, irrespective of the circumstances of its creation, irrespective of the circumstances of its birth, irrespective of the conditions that they find themselves in life, in a planet where life is increasingly not valued, in a planet where people are summarily discarded, all life is worthy of protection, and all life enjoys God's love." Energized by his passionate defense of life, I asked him in 2013 to lead the fight in the Senate for the Pain-Capable Unborn Child Protection Act. Surprisingly, he declined. He had been burned by an earlier failed effort to move forward on an immigration reform bill and was reluctant to take the lead on this issue without "all the ducks being in a row," including unrealistic assurances about possible future constitutional rulings on the issue.

The senator who did accept the challenge—Senator Lindsey Graham of South Carolina—also ran for president in 2016. Graham was bold, saying, "They can debate all day and night about the Constitution, but let's just see how they vote." That contagious confidence combined with prudent risk-taking is part of what makes Senator Graham an effective legislator, adept at crossing party lines for the sake of the cause. He has become a very good friend. He had previously championed a law to designate children in utero as victims if they are injured or killed during the commission of a federal crime. Graham instinctively knows good strategy and how to communicate the extremism and perversity of late-term abortion. He spoke at the SBA List gala in 2015, saying, "There are seven countries who allow wholesale abortions at the five-month period. I don't want to be in that club. I am dying to have this debate. I am dying to talk about who we are in America, what makes us special as a country. I am dying to hear from the other side how this makes America a better place."

One 2016 candidate for whom I had high hopes was Wisconsin's governor, Scott Walker. It took political courage for him to confront the public employee unions in Wisconsin and political skill for him to survive a brutal recall election. He had a pro-life record as governor and had defunded Planned Parenthood in his state—so it was surprising to me that when we asked him to commit to endorsing a late-term abortion ban nationally and at the state level, he demurred. Even some of the pro-life movement's strongest advocates had grown susceptible to an ill-advised "truce" strategy first suggested by former Indiana governor Mitch Daniels. It was in fact no truce at all—rather, it was an insidious, demoralizing call for unilateral surrender by pro-lifers and social conservatives so that political leaders could focus on more "urgent" issues like deficit reduction and the economy. Faulty though it was, it effectively sowed doubts and fears among even the best—and we were proposing something that was, at the time, new and untested.

I remember meeting Walker in a television network greenroom as we crossed paths before and after our respective interviews. I urged him to publicly support the bill banning abortions after five months of pregnancy that was making its way through the Wisconsin legislature and the one advancing on the national level. He deflected by saying, "People back home aren't talking about this." Soon after, on March 1, 2015, he gave an incoherent answer on abortion to anchor Chris Wallace during an interview on *Fox News Sunday*. After a swift and public response from pro-life leaders in Wisconsin and nationally, Walker came out in favor of the five-month abortion ban. In spite of the convincing it took, I believe he—like Rubio—was sincerely on board with the principle of the Pain-Capable bill as an entirely reasonable piece of legislation long before he came to embrace its strategic value. Their stories illustrate the power of the pro-life movement to overcome fear and bring even our friends back from the brink when they are faltering. Rubio and Walker are, and will always be, two of our greatest champions.

Another candidate seduced by the "truce" strategy was Governor John Kasich of Ohio. Like Walker, Kasich has a long pro-life record stretching back more than thirty years. He agreed to the commitments we asked him to make and signed a state-level version of the Pain-Capable bill banning abortions after five months. But on the campaign trail, he never seemed to miss an opportunity to downplay the significance of the pro-life issue, listing it as just one among many, on par with education and the environment. I wrote in the summer of 2015,

At a New Hampshire town hall yesterday, Gov. Kasich said that *Roe v. Wade* is "the law of the land now" and that "we live by the law of the land."

Kasich offered no other comments after being asked about his stance on abortion, and quickly pivoted to another question. This comes on the heels of remarks the Governor made on CNN criticizing Republicans for focusing "too much" on abortion.

Governor Kasich begs the question. America is aware of the law. It allows abortion up until birth. Pro-life voters, especially most Republican primary voters, do not accept *Roe* as the law of the land. Its assault on federal and states' rights to protect unborn children claims over 3,000 unborn boys and girls and their mothers as victims every day.

Primary voters will benefit from understanding Governor Kasich's policy agenda when it comes to abortion. Right now it appears he is satisfied with *Roe's* status quo: abortion on-demand up until the moment of birth.

Most of the other candidates for the Republican nomination were pro-life champions of long standing who endorsed our top legislative priorities without reservation. Senator Ted Cruz of Texas, a skilled litigator, was a particularly effective advocate, as was Senator Rand Paul of Kentucky. Former governors Rick Perry of Texas, Mike Huckabee of Arkansas, and Bobby Jindal of Louisiana all led effective pro-life administrations. Even Governor

Chris Christie of New Jersey, not often thought of as a social conservative, defunded Planned Parenthood in his state multiple times and signed on to SBA List's national agenda. Ben Carson, who emerged as a conservative favorite during the Obama administration, brought a unique perspective to the abortion debate based on his experience as a pediatric neurosurgeon. I met him several times and introduced him to a large gathering of top conservative leaders, and I came away convinced of his purity of heart and his rock-solid commitment to the unborn. Former Pennsylvania senator Rick Santorum was a prolife hero who led the fight in the Senate in 2003 for the Partial Birth Abortion Ban Act; he eagerly agreed to our legislative priorities.

For SBA List, one candidate was a particular favorite. Carly Fiorina, the dynamic former CEO of Hewlett-Packard, was the ideal pro-life spokeswoman—the kind of candidate we could only have dreamed of when SBA List was founded in 1992. Carly smartly and directly took on the flawed feminism of the proabortion movement and exposed the lie at the center of its philosophy—a lie that pits women against their own children and says for one to thrive, the other must die.

The SBA List staff and our donors loved Carly's message, and why not? It was exactly the message we had been founded to promote. Even though we knew Carly's path to victory was steep, it was easy to encourage her efforts and be excited about her campaign. As the debates got underway, Carly aggressively and effectively exposed the

ugly truth behind Planned Parenthood's abortion business and its gruesome traffic in the body parts of aborted
babies; her clear and fearless witness to the truth attracted
new followers and energized our movement. Her voice
was indispensable.

Carly pressed us for an endorsement, and she was
right to do so. Ultimately, we had to acknowledge that
SBA List's mission had grown beyond solely supporting
pro-life women candidates. For all her many impressive
strengths, in a field this crowded, Fiorina was unable to
raise the money she needed to win the nomination. Still,
I and many on our team continued to root for her success
and cheer her on.

Virtually all the candidates in the Republican primary
campaign were known quantities—people with public
records and long histories of support for the right to
life. We had experience working with them to achieve
goals we shared; although some were more committed
than others, all had agreed to support our legislative
priorities.

And then there was Donald Trump.

I didn't take his candidacy seriously at first. Trump had
been making noise about running for years. I couldn't
believe he would give up his business empire and all it
entailed to enter a political campaign in which he would
be outmatched (I thought) by far more experienced
competitors.

In the weeks leading up to his formal announcement
on June 16, 2015, my disinterest turned to alarm. All

the other Republican presidential candidates, despite their differences on issues ranging from the economy to immigration to foreign policy, were united behind our legislative priorities. Would Donald Trump make the same commitments? And if he did, could we trust him? I doubted it.

In the early days of Trump's candidacy, I learned a couple of things that tempered my skepticism. In years past, prior to her work with Senator Ted Cruz's super PAC, my friend and SBA List's longtime pollster Kellyanne Conway had briefed Trump on pro-life issues. On July 22, 2015, Trump released a statement to Christian Broadcasting Network's David Brody saying, "I support the Pain-Capable Unborn Child Protection Act and urge Congress to pass this bill. A ban on elective abortions after 20 weeks will protect unborn children. We should not be one of seven countries that allow elective abortions after 20 weeks. It goes against our core values."

I was thrilled with Trump's endorsement of the Pain-Capable bill but still questioned his sincerity and doubted he would ever agree to defund Planned Parenthood. Around that time, I learned that Chuck Laudner, a well-known GOP political operative who shepherded Rick Santorum's campaign to victory in the Iowa caucus in 2012, was heading up Trump's campaign in Iowa. I was flabbergasted. Laudner always worked for the biggest pro-life candidate—what was he doing supporting Donald Trump?

I called Chuck one afternoon from home; the intense conversation I had while sitting on my living room sofa certainly got the attention of my family. I pressed him repeatedly for specifics. What exactly will Trump do for the unborn? Will he champion pro-life issues? Is he going to defund Planned Parenthood? For his part, Chuck was upset by my questions, as if I were questioning his own pro-life bona fides. But all he would say is "I think you are going to be happy, later." I was exasperated. "Later? What does that mean? Why can't you just tell me now?"

A couple of hours later, I got my answer. SBA List's communications director, Mallory Quigley, called me and asked, "Did you see what Trump told Fox News anchor Chris Wallace?" He told him that he favored defunding Planned Parenthood. I began to realize that with Trump, there was more than meets the eye. Wallace asked if Trump would be willing to shut down the federal government over the issue of Planned Parenthood funding. He replied, "I do not want to say that because I want to show unpredictability. You have to. You can't just go around and say that. But Planned Parenthood should absolutely be defunded. I mean, if you look at what's going on with that, it's terrible."

I appreciated Trump's willingness to align with the pro-life cause, but the crass and demeaning things he said about women often offended me and those of the women voters we sought to mobilize. I was at the first Republican primary debate in Cleveland, Ohio, in August 2015, and although I applauded Trump's statement that he had "evolved" on the issue of abortion and was pro-life, I cringed when he attacked moderator Megyn Kelly and insulted entertainer

Rosie O'Donnell. I tweeted, "Trump—it's not ok to demean women or anyone." My three daughters were very much on my mind at that moment.

At first, Trump's candidacy seemed like a distraction, but as the first caucuses and primaries approached, he was outperforming many more seasoned candidates in the polls. It was time to get worried. Along with Penny Nance of Concerned Women for America and several other women leaders, I sent an open letter to voters in Iowa and South Carolina urging them to support anyone but Trump. "America will only be a great nation when we have leaders of strong character who will defend both unborn children and the dignity of women," we wrote. "We cannot trust Donald Trump to do either. Therefore we urge our fellow citizens to support an alternative candidate." What would a Trump victory mean for our policy goals? What kind of judges could we expect him to appoint?

Our letter was offset by the endorsements Trump received from national evangelical leaders, including Jerry Falwell Jr., who seemed not to share our misgivings. At the same time, Trump was doing things we had to take note of. He was communicating profoundly pro-life statements and positions.

Trump's public statements on the abortion issue, while sometimes unpolished, were often more compelling than those of many practiced politicians. In January 2016, to mark the forty-third anniversary of the Supreme Court's decision in *Roe v. Wade*, Trump authored an op-ed published by the *Washington Examiner* in which he wrote, "The Supreme Court in 1973 based its decision on imagining rights and liberties in the Constitution that are nowhere to be found." He continued,

> Over time, our culture of life in this country has started sliding toward a culture of death. Perhaps the most significant piece of evidence to support this assertion is that since *Roe v. Wade* was decided by the Supreme Court 43 years ago, over 50 million Americans never had the chance to enjoy the opportunities offered by this country. They never had the chance to become doctors, musicians, farmers, teachers, husbands, fathers, sons or daughters. They never had the chance to enrich the culture of this nation or to bring their skills, lives, loves or passions into the fabric of this country. They are missing, and they are missed.

A few weeks later, in response to the unexpected death on February 13 of Supreme Court Justice Antonin Scalia, Trump tweeted that his death was a "massive setback" for the conservative movement. Shortly thereafter, he made an extraordinary commitment to appoint only pro-life judges "in the mold" of Justice Scalia—the most explicit pro-life pledge made by any candidate for presidential office in American history.

In early March, I participated in a panel discussion with Russell Moore, the leader of the Southern Baptist Convention's Ethics and Religious Liberty Commission. He stated emphatically that Trump was the only unacceptable candidate. Moore objected not to Trump's policy positions but to his personal behavior and demeanor. I countered that we were not going to find the ideal candidate, and the only criterion by which we could judge was the specificity and believability of the policy commitments a candidate made. I knew too many genteel politicians who had betrayed our trust.

As March came to a close, it became clearer that Trump could be the nominee of the Republican Party and potentially president. During a March 30 televised town hall meeting in Wisconsin, Trump was pressed by moderator Chris Matthews on the abortion issue. What consequences, if any, should women face for having an abortion? In a lengthy exchange in which Trump effectively challenged Matthews, a Catholic, to defend his support for legal abortion in opposition to his church's teaching that it is a moral evil, Trump indicated an openness to imposing penalties on women who obtained abortions if *Roe v. Wade* were overturned. His position was at odds with that of the pro-life movement—and was quickly corrected to say that the penalties should apply to the abortionists rather than the vulnerable women who are often victims themselves. While I disagreed with Trump's answer, I recognized it as an answer that was consistent with the zeal of a convert. It was clear that in his own mind, he had wrestled with the issue and had come to the conclusion that abortion was morally wrong. It causes the deaths of children, and there must be consequences. He had just not yet come to know that the woman is also a victim of abortion, as the pro-life movement has argued for decades.

One by one, more experienced, well-funded, and politically savvy competitors abandoned their campaigns. Donald Trump would be the Republican nominee. He reached the delegate threshold to clinch the nomination in late May 2016. Many political pundits and elected officials, including Senator Ted Cruz, were still having trouble grasping the reality of what had happened, but it was abundantly clear to me and our team at SBA List that November's election would be a choice between Donald Trump and Hillary Clinton. I still had misgivings about Trump and questioned whether he would follow through on his promises. But I had absolutely no doubt that Hillary Clinton would do exactly what she had promised, which would mean—among other things—Supreme Court appointments that would close the door on any chance to overturn *Roe v. Wade* for a generation or more.

On June 21, 2016, I attended a closed-door meeting of several hundred religious leaders and social conservatives organized by Bill Dallas in New York City at which Trump asked for our endorsements. I also met with him privately in a much smaller group. He was accompanied by two pro-life champions, former Arkansas governor Mike Huckabee and Dr. Ben Carson, both former primary opponents, and was introduced by two leaders of the evangelical Christian community, Jerry Falwell Jr. and Franklin Graham, son of the Rev. Billy Graham. Trump spoke of his Christian faith and reiterated his pro-life commitments. Almost in spite of myself, I came away impressed by the man and his unapologetic embrace of the fundamental right to life for the unborn. I had witnessed so many politicians hedge the issue over the years that it was refreshing to hear someone speak in such plain and forceful language. I joined a handful of other leaders, including the Family Research Council's Tony Perkins, at a press conference following the meeting. As the only woman, the majority of the questions seemed to come to me. I expressed how encouraged I was by Trump's pro-life commitments and said I could in good conscience vote for him over Hillary, given her proabortion extremism. But I also made clear that we would need much more to mobilize our donors and our grassroots network to vote for Trump in November.

The campaign asked me if I would be the chairman of the pro-life coalition for Trump. By this time, Kellyanne Conway was the campaign manager and Sarah Huckabee Sanders—Mike's daughter and a savvy campaigner—senior advisor. I began talking with Kellyanne about something that went to the heart of Donald Trump's core competency: making a deal. I told them that I could take on this role if the pro-life movement received in writing a commitment to our top priorities. We in turn would distribute that written pledge through all our grassroots networks, including door to door in swing states. We sent a draft of a letter to the campaign and waited. We contacted many different people in the campaign to see if and when anyone would respond; frankly, it wasn't always clear who had the ability to get things done.

While we waited, Trump made a decision that put to rest the most urgent concern I and others in the pro-life movement had about his candidacy—his choice of Indiana governor Mike Pence as his running mate. As a congressman, Pence led the effort to defund Planned Parenthood; as governor of Indiana, he signed a dozen pro-life initiatives into law. I urged Mike Pence to run for president in 2012; he chose instead to run for governor of his home state. At an event in 2015 in Ohio organized by Nathan Estruth, Pence talked with a small group of SBA List members. He told them about the time he and his wife, Karen, were considering a run for Congress. He wanted his three children to understand the sacrifices they would make and why the sometimes lonely road was the only one to take. Karen and Mike showed them a picture of a developing unborn child and said, "This is why [we run]." Pence was, and is, a true pro-life warrior. I spoke on the phone with Governor Pence shortly after he was announced as Trump's choice. It was a profoundly humbling moment to realize that it was Donald Trump to whom I owed my gratitude.

On the night of Pence's acceptance speech to the Republican convention, I was in the convention arena in Cleveland and watched Senator Ted Cruz take the stage and refuse to endorse the ticket. I was shocked he would pull what I considered a cheap stunt. Walking out of the arena, I spoke with *Washington Post* reporter David Weigel to vent. "Why is he the only one who gets to be pure?" I asked. "You don't come to a Republican convention, where the whole point is to galvanize support for the nominee, and not endorse." As I told another reporter that evening, "It presumes upon the future to think that we can disengage now. I think it assumes that future generations will somehow bring the court back in ways that we can't possibly know or expect. . . . What we have to do is the best we can do." Cruz could step back and feel good about himself, I supposed. He fed the gathering media storm, and the job of those of us who had to get voters to the polls to defeat Hillary Clinton had just been made more difficult.

The selection of Mike Pence as vice president made it easier to mobilize the grassroots. Pence's longtime aide and ally Marc Short was a consultant to SBA List; he helped develop our 2016 organizational strategy. Marc knew, as I did, that with enough funding, the pro-life movement could be the decisive voting bloc in a winning campaign. Trump may have been a recent convert to the pro-life cause, but Mike and Karen Pence had been there from the very beginning.

But we still were waiting for the written commitments we needed from Donald Trump. July came and went. I called David Bossie, Trump's deputy campaign manager, and told him, "We don't have to do this, but we want to, and the only way for us to get this done is to get the letter." Bossie, passionately committed to the cause and the pro-life campaign role, assured us Trump would sign. So did Alan Cobb, now the campaign's coalitions director. Then I heard from Kellyanne Conway. "I've talked to Mr. Trump, and he wants to sign," she said. "But he thinks the letter should be stronger and begin with a description of how terrible Hillary is on life." We swiftly amended the letter:

September 2016

Dear Pro-Life Leader:

I am writing to invite you to join my campaign's Pro-Life Coalition, which is being spearheaded by long-time leader Marjorie Dannenfelser.

As we head into the final stretch of the campaign, the help of leaders like you is essential to ensure that pro-life voters know where I stand, and also know where my opponent, Hillary Clinton, stands.

Hillary Clinton not only supports abortion on-demand for any reason, but she'd take it a step further: she wants to force the taxpayers to pay for abortions by repealing the bi-partisan Hyde Amendment. Hillary Clinton also supports abortion until an hour before birth. And she will only appoint Supreme Court justices who share this view.

She doesn't even try to hide her extremism. When asked on *Meet the Press* when unborn children have constitutional rights, Clinton bluntly responded, "The unborn person doesn't have constitutional rights." She is so committed to this view that she proclaimed in a speech that "religious beliefs . . . have to be changed" in order to advance her abortion agenda.

Hillary Clinton's unwavering commitment to advancing taxpayer-funded abortion on-demand stands in stark contrast to the commitments I've made to advance the rights of unborn children and their mothers when elected president.

I am committed to:

Nominating pro-life justices to the U.S. Supreme Court.

Signing into law the Pain-Capable Unborn Child Protection Act, which would end painful late-term abortions nationwide.

Defunding Planned Parenthood as long as they continue to perform abortions, and re-allocating their funding to community health centers that provide comprehensive health care for women.

Making the Hyde Amendment permanent law to protect taxpayers from having to pay for abortions.

Your help is crucial to make this contrast clear in the minds of pro-life voters, especially those in battleground states. Together we can form this vital coalition so that Mike Pence and I can be advocates for the unborn and their mothers every day we are in the White House.

Sincerely,

Donald J. Trump

For twenty-five years, SBA List had been trying to convince political leaders and their campaigns that embracing a pro-life agenda was a popular, politically beneficial position that could help win elections. This claim was backed up by polling and years of experience on the ground. Yet so many politicians, with 2012 presidential nominee Mitt Romney a prime example, tried to obscure their pro-life stance, speaking of it only when forced to, and then in whispered, almost embarrassed tones. Even those whose pro-life convictions were built on principle rather than pragmatism were often reluctant to speak out. Donald Trump was the exact opposite. He fully embraced the "pro-life" identity. He wasn't going to hide his commitments—he was going to trumpet them far and wide.

Trump's letter motivated our donors, our door-to-door canvassers, and our staff. It made it possible for us to commit with conviction and confidence to the Trump campaign.

As SBA List went to work to elect Trump and Pence, we had to fend off legitimate questions from voters, political activists, and most of all the press about how we could go from trying to defeat Trump in the primaries to enthusiastically endorsing him. For me, it was very simple. There were two choices: Trump and Clinton. There were no circumstances under which Hillary Clinton, whose radical views included supporting abortion on demand up to the moment of a baby's birth, could ever be an acceptable choice. I couldn't read Trump's heart with certainty, but everyone could read his letter, and in it, he went further than any previous presidential candidate had gone in explicitly and publicly endorsing a pro-life agenda. In his public statements about the life issue during the campaign, Trump did not let the movement down.

But on October 7, 2016, there came an earthquake: a videotape emerged that rocked the campaign. It showed Trump speaking twelve years earlier to *Access Hollywood* host Billy Bush about women in a crude and misogynistic way. His words repulsed me. As the mother of three young women and two young men, I felt ill at the prospect of defending a man who could speak that way. My two oldest daughters hold views on many issues that diverge from my own, but on the issue of life, they unfailingly had defended the humanity of the unborn child. When Hannah, the oldest, came to me and said, "We really want to support you, Mom, but we can't support you if you help Donald Trump," I was shaken to the core. The collateral damage of Trump's words still affects our family today.

I had to take a step back. I had to imagine both Hillary Clinton and Donald Trump as decision makers in the Oval Office. I knew that Hillary would set back the pro-life movement for a generation or more. The decision in my mind hinged on whether Donald Trump would stay true to his pro-life commitments. I was genuinely torn.

Ultimately I had to accept my own public argument: Trump's commitment to the pro-life cause outweighed his offensive remarks. My daughters saw a snapshot in time and were right to be appalled. But I saw the evil that had been wrought in the decades since *Roe v. Wade*, which had ended the lives of more than fifty million pre-born babies. I was being asked not to defend Trump's past words but to support his current commitments and actions. That's the message I delivered on NPR a few days after the *Access Hollywood* tape emerged. What Trump said on that tape in 2005 was "outrageous and unacceptable," but the election was about the future. It was between Donald Trump and Hillary Clinton, and anyone who thought there was another choice was delusional.

I felt my confidence vindicated on October 19 when I watched the final presidential debate at home with my husband, Marty, and some of our children. Clinton used the very first question, about the Supreme Court and the interpretation of the Constitution, as a springboard to bring up her unqualified support for *Roe v. Wade*. Trump said he was committed to appointing pro-life justices and expected *Roe v. Wade* to be overturned. When moderator Chris Wallace pressed Clinton on the issue of late-term abortion, she reiterated her unequivocal belief that an unborn child has no constitutional rights at any stage of development. Then came this extraordinary response by Donald Trump:

> Well, I think it's terrible. If you go with what Hillary is saying, in the ninth month, you can take the baby and rip the baby out of the womb of the mother just prior to the birth of the baby. Now, you can say that that's OK, and Hillary can say that that's OK. But it's not OK with me, because based on what she's saying,

and based on where she's going, and where she's been, you can take the baby and rip the baby out of the womb in the ninth month on the final day. And that's not acceptable.

Finally! SBA List had made "going on offense" the theme of our candidate trainings. I had counseled dozens of candidates from the presidential level down to the state legislature. Not one did a better job of communicating the visceral horror of abortion. Mitt Romney, John McCain, George W. Bush, even Ronald Reagan had been given on a national stage many opportunities to authentically witness to the depravity and extremism of abortion; all had shied away. Only Donald Trump had the courage to speak the truth to a national television audience.

The entire SBA List team went into the final weeks of the campaign with a renewed sense of enthusiasm and hope. We did everything we possibly could to win not just the presidential election but also critical Senate and House races. We deployed nearly one thousand canvassers, visited more than a million homes, and spoke to hundreds of thousands more through phones, mail, and social media. But as Election Day approached, the polls and the pundits pointed to a Clinton victory. I heard far different reports from our staff and allies on the ground, who told us of the enormous crowds turning out for Trump's rallies and the extremely positive responses that our canvassers were getting at the homes of key voters in Florida, Ohio, and North Carolina. SBA List board member Carol Moore called me a few days before the election and said, "There are fifteen thousand people turning out for a Trump rally in Florida. That never happens! Don't you see he is going to win?" I got similar reports from another board member, Rob Kania, about his home state of Pennsylvania. Our top political strategist, Frank Cannon, said he could see in the polls a path to victory, as he had said throughout the campaign. Our national field director, Tim Edson, was absolutely sure Trump would win. "What's wrong with you people?" he said. "We are definitely going to win!" I couldn't even bear to think about what a loss would mean for our mission to end legal abortion . . . or what it would cost the babies who would be aborted and their mothers. I kept thinking back to Election Day in 2012, when I had thought Romney would win only to be painfully disappointed. It seemed safer to expect the worst.

Election Day is always the worst for those of us who work at the senior level on campaigns—there's not much left to do but wait. I went to Mass that morning at St. Matthew's Cathedral near my office in Washington, DC, and sat in the church long after it was over, praying for the courage and humility to accept the result if Clinton prevailed. As I walked back to the office, I called Marc Short, who was with Mike Pence. "What are the odds?" I asked. He never gave me a number, but I knew him well enough to know he was worried.

That evening, as our friends, families, and staff all gathered at our headquarters in Washington, we watched with apprehension as the returns started to come in. The early results from Virginia were not good. It was not a state we'd campaigned in but one we had hoped to win. The early returns from Florida, Ohio, and North Carolina were all too close to call. We believed we needed to win each of those states in order to have a fighting chance. The hours that passed by were excruciating. As the night dragged on, and the numbers were crunched, we began to believe the impossible. The victory in Wisconsin was the turning point, followed by Michigan . . . then Pennsylvania! Hillary's path to victory was narrowing, while Trump's was expanding. As gloom descended upon most TV commentators, the mood lifted in our little pro-life command center. At nearly 3 a.m., the race was finally called, and Trump came out on stage to claim his victory. Not only had Trump won, but thirty-three of the thirty-nine House and Senate candidates we endorsed won as well. President Trump would have a governing majority—a judicial game plan was made possible with a pro-life Senate and presidency and a mission-liberating night like no other.

The 2016 election was a watershed for the pro-life movement. Voters rejected Hillary Clinton's bankrupt vision of a feminist future in which women are at war with their own children. Clinton campaigned on the most radical abortion platform in history. For the first time, the Democratic Party platform ratified in 2016 explicitly called for the repeal of the Hyde Amendment, advocating direct taxpayer funding for abortion and the repeal of any federal or state restriction on abortion up to birth. In a speech at a Women of the World summit in 2015, Clinton said that "deep-seated cultural codes, religious beliefs and structural biases have to be changed" to expand abortion on demand. Later she labeled half of America "irredeemable" and "deplorable." Her defeat was a blow that proabortion elites did not see coming and a welcome reprieve to many who'd been trampled underneath the Far Left's cultural agenda.

The next morning, though, our work began anew. We had Trump's commitments. We were in part responsible for Trump's victory by reassuring pro-life voters that he would follow through on them. Now we had to make sure he delivered. Many of our strongest and longtime friends—including Bill Kristol, Robby George, Russell Moore, John McCormack, and other allies—believed we were wrong to support Donald Trump. We now had to set about the transformative work we'd striven to make possible. And it would be clear how wrong they were not to support him.

There was time, though, to work through all these concerns. First I had to catch up on the things I neglected during the campaign—including sleep. A couple of weeks after the election, while I was taking a nap, a message was left on my cell phone. It said,

> Hi, Marjorie. I want to thank you for the great job you did. It was amazing. Everybody's talking about it. They say you knocked on one million doors. Boy, that's a lot of doors! So you and your group—and I

want to just thank you, thank all of the people that were with you, and we'll never forget. You are incredible; everyone's talking about you. So I just wanted to leave you a little message, and thank you, Marjorie, 'cause . . . the job you did was incredible, and, uh, sort of record setting. And it's been a great victory, and you keep in touch. We really appreciate it. Thanks. Thanks a lot, Marjorie. Bye.

It took me a minute to comprehend who had left the message. It was the man who had the potential to be the greatest pro-life champion ever elected president: Donald J. Trump.

CHAPTER 3

"What If I've Been Wrong?"

I LOVE THE SONG "AMERICAN Honey" by Lady Antebel-lum. Every time I hear the opening words—"She grew up on a side of the road / Where church bells ring and strong love grows"—I am transported back to my home-town of Greenville, North Carolina, and to a childhood in which I was allowed to grow up, as the song says, "good and slow." It is a precious gift to know who you are and where you are from, and I am grateful.

My mother, Hannah—everyone calls her Hansy—Warren was born and raised in Greenville, and it was her roots that drew my parents there after my father's stint as an Army doctor ended in 1967. My mom met Billy Jones on a blind date when she was an undergraduate at Duke and he was at Duke's medical school. They loved the Army life, but after having three children in three different cit-ies, they were ready to put down roots. I was an infant when my parents settled in Greenville. My father set up a private practice as a dermatologist, and my mother later went back to school to pursue her master's degree in library science.

Greenville is a quiet and pretty college town, the home of Eastern Carolina University, nestled in an area rich in history and blessed with natural beauty. But for me, the best part of Greenville was that my maternal grand-mother lived there. Hannah Fulford Warren was smart, feminine, and a woman of the South—soft and kind on the outside, strong as steel on the inside. My grandfather died in 1964, leaving my grandmother and her formida-ble sisters, Alice and Maud, also widows, to their own devices.

I loved sitting among these women as they talked about their childhood growing up in Hertford, North Caro-lina, on the banks of the Perquimans River, and later in Washington, North Carolina, where their father started a hardware store. His venture flourished for a while, then faltered, and the family moved again, this time to Greenville. My grandmother and aunts all taught school before they married. I was amused by their tales of need-ing a male escort to walk downtown and being courted by suitors in the parlor of their college dormitory. It seemed like they had come from another world—which, in a way, they had. I absorbed their Episcopal faith, quiet and strong, and their love for church liturgy and hymns. But the best thing about being with my aunts and especially my grandmother was that they loved me unconditionally and made sure I knew it.

I vividly remember counting the days until I could join my older brothers at Wahl-Coates Elementary School. As the youngest child and only girl, I was desperate to tag along any time they would let me. I did not know that Greenville's schools had a legacy of discrimination, nor did I know of the court orders that had been issued to force the city to rectify that injustice. In 1970, sixteen years after the Supreme Court's decision in *Brown v. Board of Education*, Judge John Larkins of the U.S. District Court for the Eastern District of North Carolina found that Greenville continued to "unlawfully operate and maintain racially segregated schools." On July 31, 1970, he approved a plan to bus students to establish a ratio of white to black students in elementary schools of two to one—roughly the ratio in the city as a whole. And so in September 1971, instead of walking to my neighborhood school, I boarded a bus at the corner of our street and traveled across town to start first grade.

Many of the families in our neighborhood reacted to the court order by sending their children to private or religious schools. Only a few of my brother's friends from Wahl-Coates Elementary joined us on the bus that fall. For my parents, there was never any question that we would willingly comply. They weren't activists—far from it—but it was clear to them, and therefore to me, that school segregation in Greenville was wrong and needed to end and that the fastest way to do it was through the force of the law requiring busing to achieve racial balance.

At the age of six, I was only vaguely aware of the social changes taking place around me. I went to elementary school with my brothers as I had so long desired, and I loved it. As I got older, I came to understand the grave injustice busing was meant to remedy. When I entered first grade, the only person I knew in town who was African American was my babysitter, Martha; she had attended Greenville's public schools for a while but could not read or write. Separate was definitely *not* equal for children growing up in Greenville in those days.

As one student among thousands who were part of an effort that was (and still is) messy, difficult, and imperfect, I had my first experience of what it takes to right a deeply entrenched wrong. It is easy to give an inspirational speech; it is satisfying to participate in a march or protest. These things are good and have their place. But real change is hard and takes time. I also learned in a very direct way the power of the law as a teacher of what is right and acceptable in society. I don't know when, if ever, Greenville's schools would have desegregated if Judge Larkins hadn't ordered them to do so, with the full weight of constitutional law behind his decree.

The issues raised by the civil rights movement of the 1960s and 1970s were integral to my experience growing up in a small Southern town still grappling with a shameful history of racial discrimination. In contrast, the feminist movement unfolding at the same time was more remote. My mother and father were firm believers in family dinner discussions that focused on big issues rather than the mundane news of the day, and "women's lib" was one of our regular topics. We debated the Equal Rights Amendment and the justice of equal pay for equal work and celebrated new opportunities opening up for women in law, medicine, science, and government. My parents were conservative in their economic and foreign policy views and were registered Republicans. One issue we did not need to debate: my parents thought abortion was a necessary evil, and so did I.

In 1984 I followed in my parents' footsteps and headed off to Duke University. I was interested in politics but planned on a career in medicine, like my father. (My terrible performance in premed science classes ultimately led me to abandon that path!) When I arrived on campus for freshman orientation, however, the main thought on my mind was that I might be pregnant. For me at that time, there was only one option, and it didn't involve leaving school and having a baby. Thankfully, it was just a scare. But the fear I felt at that moment is something I will never forget. I experienced the terror and loneliness of an unsure future and confused shame of embracing but fearing an abortion and folks knowing about it. I felt the fury that arose from the deepest part of me that anyone would believe that they had a role in my decision—that any self-righteous stranger thought they could plan my life.

Permanently etched in my memory is the phone call I made from the Bryan Student Center to find out the results of my pregnancy test. What I remember most are the moments before, standing at the top of the escalator, gaining the courage to call while other students were going through the exciting and mundane tasks of moving in, buying books at the "Book Ex," meeting roommates, and looking forward to orientation. I was determined that, no matter what, I would live out the same experience as them—not one that included isolation and the unheard-of path of a freshman and mother. I would also *not* go through the humiliating ordeal of withdrawing on the first day of college.

I made the phone call in the little booth next to the information desk. The result was negative. Ahhh—the clouds parted. I buried the whole trial. For a while.

Soon after I arrived at Duke, I joined the College Republicans and threw myself into efforts to reelect President Ronald Reagan in November. Like so many young people who came of age in the 1980s, I admired President Reagan for his policies and his personality. In a sign of how divided the Republican Party was on the issue of abortion (and in contrast to its unity on economics, the role of government, and foreign policy), Duke's College Republicans had two leaders—one pro-life, another pro-choice. From pro-life chairman Tim Neeley and his allies, I heard for the first time a principled and coherent argument against abortion on legal and moral grounds. But *I* was the pro-*choice* chairman and could not be persuaded otherwise. When Dr. Bernard Nathanson's film *The Silent Scream* was shown on campus, I refused to go—I said it was "offensive." My oh-so-clever line to men who disagreed with me? "When you become a woman, come back and talk to me." How deaf I was to the voices of the unborn children, boys and girls, whose lives I so cavalierly dismissed.

In the summer between my junior and senior years, I worked as an intern at the Heritage Foundation, a think tank in Washington, DC. Heritage was widely seen as playing an instrumental role in advancing Reagan's ideas, and I was thrilled to be a part of the cause. I lived in a co-ed group house on O Street in Georgetown that was dubbed the "Right House" because everyone who lived there was a conservative. But it took only a few days in Washington for me to realize that the word *conservative* meant different things to different people, and the divides went beyond the simple pro-life/pro-choice labels used at Duke. Was I a libertarian? A supply-sider? A neo-con? A member of the "religious right"? Did I favor a "big tent" or ideological purity? It seemed that everywhere I turned, I was being asked to define, and then defend, what I believed.

The debates in the Right House were a microcosm of those being played out that summer on a larger stage in the Republican primaries to choose a successor to Reagan. Some of my housemates were libertarians, skeptical of state power and committed to individual autonomy. Like me, they were mostly pro-choice. Others were traditional and social conservatives who supported limited government and a strong defense and regarded *Roe v. Wade* as a tragic betrayal of our nation's founding principles. Over the course of the summer, I was constantly challenged—at first in the kind of long, boozy, overwrought debates college students from the beginning of time have engaged in and later in a more serious and systematic way—to define what I believed and why.

In this effort, I had many guides, but none more important than the example set by my mother and grandmother. I admired them in many things, but most of all for their authenticity. They taught me that the only way to know myself was to ask questions, seek truth, and not deceive myself about the answers; they gave me the courage to take risks to find the truth.

In his classic *Mere Christianity*, C. S. Lewis writes,

> Every time you make a choice you are turning the central part of you, the part of you that chooses, into something a little different than it was before. And taking your life as a whole, with all your innumerable choices, all your life long you are slowly turning this central thing into a heavenly creature or a hellish creature: either into a creature that is in harmony with God, and with other creatures, and with itself, or else into one that is in a state of war and hatred with God, and with its fellow creatures, and with *itself*. To be the one kind of creature is heaven: that is, it is joy and peace and knowledge and power. To be the other means madness, horror, idiocy, rage, impotence, and eternal loneliness. Each of us at each moment is progressing to the one state of the other.

And so it was that many little choices along the way had led me to a point of choosing that would orient my life from that day forward.

The impetus was what might seem a trivial thing—a dispute in the Right House about an arguably pornographic video. Dean Clancy found it in the VCR and destroyed it; Mike Centanni, a libertarian who was the house manager (and was convicted in 2015 on charges of possessing child pornography) demanded that Dean pay for it. The fight escalated, and what it revealed was a deep schism, two fundamentally different ways of looking at the world and our place in it. Dean and his friends were devout Catholics who believed pornography to be an evil that violated human dignity and harmed the community as a whole. The libertarians were more utilitarian; to them the issue was about property rights and freedom of speech, and they were not about to ban something they believed was a matter of individual choice. The libertarians had control of the house and forced Dean and those who agreed with him to leave.

I wasn't aligned at that point with either group; I could have stayed in the Right House. But as I listened to the debate, something stirred within me, and I knew what was at stake was more fundamental than where I would sleep for the next several weeks. I chose to leave.

Dean's arguments, and those of our friend Chris Currie, were rooted not in politics but in deeper truths about the human person that came from their Catholic faith. I, too, was a Christian believer; I loved the Episcopal Church in which I had been raised. But when I went looking for answers to the moral questions that confronted me that summer, it seemed my church had nothing compelling to say.

What a contrast to the witness of the Catholic Church as I encountered it through Jesuit priests like Father Robert Spitzer and Father Joseph Durkin, who were friends and mentors to Chris, Dean, and others I knew. Chris remains the best apologist for the Catholic faith I've met. Through them, I was introduced to a church led by Pope John Paul II, who wrote in *Familiaris Consortio* that "God gives man and woman an equal personal dignity, endowing them with the inalienable rights and responsibilities proper to the human person" but that "the dignity of women is contradicted by that persistent mentality which considers the human being not as a person but as a thing, as an object of trade, at the service of selfish interest and mere pleasure," a mentality that "produces very bitter fruits, such as contempt for men and for women, slavery, oppression of the weak, pornography, prostitution . . . and all those various forms of discrimination that exist in the fields of education, employment, [and] wages." I have never encountered a more compelling call for women's rights. This same pope told the General Assembly of the United Nations, "Concern for the child, even before birth, from the first moment of conception and then throughout the years of infancy and youth, is the primary and fundamental test of the relationship of one human being to another." In Pope John Paul II, I encountered the Catholic Church's rich anthropology rooted in the natural rights and inherent dignity of every human person at every stage of development, from conception to natural death. What a profound challenge he offered to my pro-choice convictions!

That summer I made a decision about my view on abortion. Combining all the things that occurred that summer—the death of a childhood friend, what I read about women and children in faith, what I was learning about the consequences of belief, and feeling a call to leadership and a new direction—I made a decision to change my view on abortion from strongly pro-choice to strongly pro-life. I went back to Duke that fall with many unresolved questions about my faith and future. I looked for answers in my studies in philosophy, immersing myself in the wisdom of the ancients and medievals. But on the issue of abortion, I was decided. Soon after returning, I started a pro-life club and wrote a letter to the editor of the school newspaper. Identifying myself as a former pro-choice chair of the College Republicans, I asked a simple question: What if I've been wrong? What if our nation is wrong? The price of our nation being wrong was the lives of millions of innocents each year.

My former adversaries embraced me far more than my former allies rejected me. But I didn't raise the issue with my parents for a long time. With them, my conversion on the issue of abortion was tied up with a much deeper one: the Catholic faith. I returned to Washington, DC, after I graduated from Duke; went to work again at the Heritage Foundation; and began formal preparations with Father Durkin to enter the Catholic Church. Whenever I did talk to my parents about abortion, they made it clear they disagreed; they still do.

They were unsettled by my decision to become a Catholic but respected my agency on the matter and came to accept and respect it. I found it hard to leave the Episcopal

Church—it was so tied up with who I was and where I belonged that I felt like I was leaving myself behind. In a way, I was. But my family had taught me to follow the truth wherever it led, and it led me to my true home.

My parents came to the Mass where I was received into the Church at Pentecost in 1989. At the invitation of the saintly Father Durkin, who continually praised the "beautiful Episcopal Church," they were the only ones who sang.

CHAPTER 4

The Great Unfilled Need

THE HERITAGE FOUNDATION WAS the hub of the conservative movement, and in the summer of 1989,
it was still a pivotal player in the Reagan revolution of
lower taxes, smaller government, and a strong national
defense it helped usher in. Heritage was a testing ground
for ideas, and I had a front-row seat as its experts and
political allies from the Hill and around the country
debated and refined the policy initiatives it hoped would
define the movement for the next generation. I loved
meeting the people who filtered in and out of Heritage's
near-constant round of receptions, speeches, and semi-
nars. Political DC was always interesting and sometimes
exciting—but it wasn't home, and home was where I
wanted to be. In the summer of 1989, I began looking
for a job in the administration of North Carolina governor Jim Martin (my first political campaign), who had
been reelected in 1988 to a second term in the Raleigh
statehouse.

There's an old saying, "If you want to hear God laugh,
tell him your plans." It was my friend Susan Smith who
set in motion the events that would upend everything I
envisioned for my future. Susan and I met at Heritage in
1987. By 1989, she was a lobbyist for the National Right

to Life Committee, the oldest and largest pro-life advocacy group in the nation at the time.

The pro-life movement's legislative priorities at the federal level in the 1980s focused primarily on restricting taxpayer-funded abortions. But the Supreme Court's five-to-four decision in July 1989 in *Webster v. Reproductive Health Services* opened the door to the possibility that more explicit restrictions on abortion might be found constitutional. The *Webster* case involved a Missouri law that placed strict limits on the use of state funds, employees, and institutions to facilitate abortion in any way. One of the law's key architects, Andrew Puzder (who later was a successful CEO and President Trump's first nominee as secretary of labor) told the *Chicago Tribune* in 1989 that the law was "designed to make the Supreme Court face the question of deciding whether a state can decide when life exists." The Missouri law's preamble stated that "the life of each human being begins at conception," and "unborn children have protectable interests in life, health, and well-being." The court punted on the law's direct challenge to *Roe v. Wade*, allowing that ruling to stand, but otherwise upheld its constitutionality. All of a sudden, the abortion issue, always simmering below the surface, was brought into sharp focus nationwide. Lawmakers in dozens of states began working to pass new laws to limit and regulate abortion, while proabortion forces mobilized to block any effort to restrain the unfettered right to abortion *Roe* had sanctioned.

The *Washington Post* reported that the *Webster* decision "transformed the abortion issue from a constitutional debate into a political struggle." This sea change threatened the fragile bipartisan majority in the U.S. House of Representatives that had held firm in support of pro-life restrictions on federal taxpayer funding despite the active hostility of Democrats who controlled both houses of Congress. It was against this backdrop that Susan asked me to consider working for West Virginia Democrat Alan Mollohan, the cochairman of the House Pro-life Caucus.

My first reaction was one of incredulity. I asked her how she could possibly ask such a question. I certainly didn't see myself making abortion the central focus of my career. Plus, Mollohan was a Democrat, and I was a Republican who wanted to continue to work for GOP candidates and officeholders. In politics, cross-party careers are very rare. A mutual friend and former colleague of Susan's and mine told me explicitly that if I took the job, I would never work in GOP politics again.

But over the course of several weeks, my perspective shifted. Early in my time at Heritage, I sought out Adam Meyerson, then the editor of its flagship journal, *Policy Review*, for career advice. He said the key to success in politics and public policy was the same as in business—start by figuring out what is missing, what needs to be done that no one else is doing, then put yourself in a position to fill that need. His advice resonated with me. This was the echo and example of my father: If it is a great need, and you can do it, do not delay. Act. As unexpected as it was, the job of organizing pro-life Democrats in an increasingly hostile House of Representatives was a job that needed doing.

I agreed to meet with Congressman Mollohan to discuss the job. In my mind, I wasn't abandoning my return to North Carolina, just postponing it. My main concern was that we wouldn't agree on any issue other than abortion. I need not have worried. Mollohan was a conservative "blue dog" Democrat representing West Virginia, and his views on most issues were to the right of many Republicans. An attorney educated at the College of William and Mary and West Virginia University, Mollohan was first elected in 1982 to a seat that had been held for more than a decade by his father. As a member of the powerful Appropriations Committee in the House, he had a direct role in determining how federal funds were spent. A devout Baptist, Mollohan opposed abortion and was a reliable pro-life vote. But a random encounter outside a restaurant on Connecticut Avenue in Washington, DC, provoked him to take on a leadership role. He told me about it the day we met in his office for my job interview. He said a stranger handed him a flyer that depicted an unborn child after an abortion. "I didn't look at the flyer right away—I just shoved it in my pocket. I planned to throw it in the trash," he said. "When I cleaned out my pockets later in the day, I looked at it, and after I gazed at that horrible reality, I knew I could no longer simply be a pro-life vote. I had to do something about it." After meeting with him, I knew I had to do something too.

And so it sunk into my soul. You cannot unknow or unsee what horror has become clear. I had to act. I started working on Capitol Hill in September 1989. Within days, I was in the midst of my first legislative battle. The Hyde Amendment was the name given to a ban, first enacted in 1976, on the use of federal Medicaid funds for abortion, except in cases where a mother's life was in danger. Named for pro-life champion Congressman Henry Hyde, it had remained in place, unchanged for more than a decade. In October 1989, as Congress considered the annual appropriation bill for the Departments of Labor and Health and Human Services, Congressman Brian Donnelly, a Democrat from Massachusetts, offered an amendment to allow Medicaid funding for abortions resulting from rape and incest. Quite unexpectedly, Donnelly's amendment passed by a vote of 216–206, with 41 Democrats and 134 Republicans voting no. The Supreme Court's decision in *Webster* had energized the abortion lobby and was rearranging the political landscape.

Abortion was not always a partisan issue. The earliest bills to legalize abortion nationwide were introduced in 1970 by Senator Bob Packwood of Oregon, a Republican. Even though several states had laws to permit abortion, the issue was not at the forefront of the 1972 presidential election. The theme of the Democrats' convention that year was later dubbed "acid, amnesty, and abortion," but their platform didn't mention the issue at the insistence of the party's nominee, Senator George McGovern of South Dakota. Both of his choices for running mate—Senator Thomas Eagleton of Missouri, who later withdrew, and his replacement, Sargent Shriver, former head of the Peace Corps—were strongly pro-life. (They were the last national Democratic Party leaders to be so.) The Republican platform likewise was silent.

Most politicians in both parties probably would have been happy to leave the issue of abortion to be decided by the states. But the Supreme Court's *Roe* decision in 1973 pushed the issue firmly into the national sphere, where it has been ever since. In 1976 the party platforms diverged on the issue, with the Democrats saying it was "undesirable" to attempt to overturn *Roe*, while Republicans said it "supports the efforts of those who seek enactment of a constitutional amendment to restore protection of the right to life for unborn children." Still, the Democratic nominee, Governor Jimmy Carter of Georgia, was an evangelical Christian who openly stated that he believed abortion was "wrong," while Republican Gerald Ford gave only tepid support to his party's platform (his wife, Betty, was a public advocate for abortion).

Hindsight, as they say, is twenty-twenty, but looking back now on the political environment in the 1970s on the issue of abortion, it seems likely that congressional action to enact limits on the unfettered abortion-on-demand regime unleashed by *Roe* would have had wide popularity in both parties. But a pro-life movement that was principled and passionate, though often scattered and disorganized, focused instead solely on the Human Life Amendment to the Constitution. Introduced in the

Senate in 1975 by Republican senators James Buckley of New York and Jesse Helms of North Carolina, it sought to overturn *Roe* by guaranteeing the right to life for all unborn persons. That initiative gained forty votes in the Senate in 1976, far short of the two-thirds majority needed to pass a constitutional amendment. No bills were even introduced to limit abortion; it was all or nothing. The only area where consensus was reached was on the federal funding of abortion. The first Hyde Amendment passed the House by a vote of 207–167, with the majority of the votes coming from Democrats, and although it was initially rejected by the Senate, it eventually became law. Its funding restrictions were later added to other federal funding streams, including in the military and federal employee health benefits.

By 1980, as Ramesh Ponnuru points out in his book *The Party of Death*, Jimmy Carter and Ronald Reagan were the "key figures in redefining the parties." Evangelicals who had supported Carter in 1976 abandoned him in 1980, driven away in part by his acceptance of *Roe*. Catholics too, who were historically part of the Democratic coalition, found themselves drawn to Reagan's message, which included the opposition to abortion. Reagan's victory in 1980 cemented a political realignment that had been brewing for a decade.

During Reagan's term, initial pro-life optimism faded when the movement split into two camps. One group, led by Senators Orrin Hatch (R-UT) and Tom Eagleton (D-MO), favored amending the Constitution in two steps, beginning with an amendment that would have returned the power to protect the unborn to the states and possibly Congress without requiring them to do so. Success would have required the approval of two-thirds of both houses of Congress and ratification by three-quarters of the states. The other proposal, the Human Life Bill proposed by Senator Jesse Helms (R-NC), would also have reversed *Roe* but used a statutory approach to protect the unborn. It would have required only a majority vote of the House and Senate.

Both measures failed in the Senate in 1982, with the constitutional amendment garnering only forty-nine votes, eighteen votes short of adoption, and the Human Life Bill failing by a single vote in mid-September. These climactic defeats helped stall pro-life momentum in the middle of Reagan's first term, and the memory of the bipartisan push that almost succeeded in national protections for the unborn has grown dim. Meanwhile, advocates of legal abortion gained sway in the Democratic Party, nominating Walter "Fritz" Mondale in 1984 and Michael Dukakis in 1988. By the late 1980s, according to Ponnuru, "Democratic politicians had been voting for abortion rights at much higher rates than Republicans. . . . Yet Democratic voters were still more pro-life than Republican voters."

This trend was playing out in real time during my first weeks on Capitol Hill. Reagan had been succeeded by his vice president, George H. W. Bush. He was a fairly recent convert on the issue of abortion, but a sincere one, calling it a "tragedy of shattering proportions." On October 23, 1989, Bush vetoed the Labor/HHS appropriations bill, writing, "I have informed the Congress on numerous occasions that I would veto legislation if it permitted the use of appropriated funds to pay for abortions other than those in which the life of the mother would be endangered." On October 25, the House attempted to override Bush's veto. After a contentious and emotional debate, the House failed to achieve the two-thirds threshold needed to override. Fifty-nine Democrats and 134 Republicans voted to sustain President Bush's veto. But in an ominous sign of shifting allegiances, Kentucky Democrat William Natcher, the chairman of the Labor/HHS Appropriations subcommittee and one of the most reliable pro-life Democrats in the House, voted to override.

The voices of proabortion women, energized in opposition to the Supreme Court's decision in *Webster*, were being heard loud and clear on Capitol Hill. On November 12, 1989, proabortion rallies were held around the nation under the slogan "Mobilize for Women's Lives." Tens of thousands of women came to Washington, DC, to lobby for the federal funding of abortion and against restrictions being enacted in the states. Two of their champions, Senator Alan Cranston and Congressman Bob Edwards, both Democrats from California, introduced a bill they called the Freedom of Choice Act (FOCA), which sought to essentially create a fundamental statutory right to abortion and criminalize measures that sought to restrict it.

A few days later, Pennsylvania Governor Bob Casey Sr., a Democrat, signed a law to outlaw abortion after the twenty-fourth week of pregnancy, except when the woman's life is severely threatened; require a twenty-four-hour waiting period before an abortion; and ban "sex-selection" abortion. The Pennsylvania law was the most extensive restriction on abortion enacted since the *Webster* decision in July. Before adjourning for the year, Congress attempted once again to overturn a long-standing prohibition on federal abortion funding, this time the Kemp-Kasten Amendment, which barred federal funding for programs that support the enforcement of China's repressive one-child-per-family policy through coercive abortion and forced sterilization. During his four-year term, Bush would have to veto ten measures that sought to expand funding for abortion.

Abortion advocates felt energized by political victories they had won in two off-year gubernatorial races in which the abortion issue played a major role. Democrats James Florio in New Jersey and Douglas Wilder in Virginia won races against pro-life opponents (although in New Jersey, the Republican congressman Jim Courter had claimed in the wake of *Webster* that he could not impose his "personal views" on New Jersey by supporting pro-life laws in the state).

In my work to organize the several dozen Democrats in the House who voted pro-life, it soon was clear the proabortion side had an advantage that pro-lifers found hard to match: a plethora of women officeholders. There were a few Republican women in the House who were pro-life—Barbara Vucanovich of Nevada and Virginia Smith of Nebraska are two examples. But not one of the Democratic women in the House—a group that included Nancy Pelosi and Barbara Boxer—was pro-life. The increasingly well-organized and militant efforts of proabortion women threatened to silence the dwindling number of members from both parties who were willing to speak out on the House floor against abortion. It didn't escape notice that their efforts were ably supported with money and muscle by EMILY's List, the new political action committee founded in 1985 with the explicit mission of electing proabortion Democratic women to Congress.

Soon after I was hired by Congressman Mollohan, I got together with my counterpart on the Republican side of the aisle. Congressman Chris Smith of New Jersey chaired the Pro-life Caucus for the Republicans, and his top aide, Marty Dannenfelser, handled the issue for him. I was in awe of Marty's encyclopedic knowledge of the pro-life movement and legislative procedure. Even more, I was attracted by his integrity, his kindness, his sense of mission, and the respect he showed to me and to everyone he met, including those with whom he disagreed. From Marty, I learned the difference between a career, which is what I thought I had, and a vocation, which is what he was living.

Marty was a cradle Catholic of a kind I had not yet encountered in my short time in the Church. I was on fire for the faith and immersed myself in Washington's

Catholic subculture of speakers, forums, and social gatherings. I invited Marty to come with me one evening after work to a lecture sponsored by the Hill's Catholic Forum. He came, and we went to dinner afterward. I saw then that he wasn't one who talked about his faith; instead, he lived it. It wasn't long before we began dating, and soon we both learned what it meant to embrace another kind of vocation—marriage.

CHAPTER 5

The Party of Abortion and the "Year of the Woman"

MARTY AND I WERE married in Greenville's tiny St. Peter's Catholic Church in April 1991. On the surface, we might have seemed an unlikely match—I was a proud Southern girl, while Marty was Bronx born and New Jersey raised, the oldest son in a large and loving Irish German family, and a "Yankee" through and through. The sedate (my mother would say "refined") wedding traditions of the South with which I had been raised mystified my soon-to-be in-laws, who were looking forward to a wedding bash with a capital *B*! But they embraced them—and me—with love and generosity. Our different backgrounds and experiences keep things interesting—and sometimes combustible—but undergirding it all is a deep unity on the things that really matter.

On Capitol Hill, where we both worked, the focus turned decisively in June 1991 to the Supreme Court. Justice Thurgood Marshall, one of the original votes for *Roe v. Wade*, announced his retirement. The vacancy gave President Bush the opportunity to appoint a successor who could be a deciding vote in a future challenge to *Roe*. On July 1, he nominated federal appeals court judge Clarence Thomas. A Yale-educated lawyer and former chairman of the Equal Employment Opportunity

Commission, Thomas was widely seen as a conservative who, like Justice Antonin Scalia, held to an originalist interpretation of the Constitution. Thomas's personal story as a descendent of slaves, raised by a single mother in Pin Point, Georgia, who overcame discrimination through hard work and personal sacrifice to attain a seat on the nation's highest court, was compelling.

The truth about who Clarence Thomas was and what he believed was quickly subsumed into a campaign of lies and distortions designed to defeat him as it had Judge Robert Bork four years earlier. The House of Representatives, where I worked, had no direct role in the confirmation process, which belonged solely to the Senate, but the pro-life movement of which I was a part mobilized in full force to support Thomas's nomination. Opponents of his nomination, not succeeding with attacks on Thomas's judicial philosophy or professional record, turned to character assassination. Judge Thomas vehemently denied Anita Hill's salacious accusations, calling the subsequent uproar a "high-tech lynching for uppity blacks who in any way deign to think for themselves, to do for themselves, to have different ideas." The controversy seemed to center on the issue of sexual harassment in the workplace, but the subtext was very clear: *Roe v. Wade* was in peril and must be defended at any cost, by any means necessary.

Thomas was confirmed by a vote of fifty-two to forty-eight on October 15, the slimmest margin for a Supreme Court justice in more than one hundred years. A few days before, on October 3, Arkansas governor Bill Clinton announced his candidacy for the Democratic presidential nomination. Clinton, the famous "triangulator" of thorny social issues, supported *Roe v. Wade* but as governor had opposed taxpayer funding and even supported a law requiring parental notification in the case of a minor seeking an abortion. In 1986, when Arkansas was considering a ban on abortion funding, Clinton wrote, "I am opposed to abortion and to government funding of abortions. We should not spend state funds on abortions because so many people believe abortion is wrong." By 1992, however, he had embraced abortion rights as well as state and federal funding. Still, he seemed to signal in his formulation that abortion should be "safe, legal, and rare" that he had moral misgivings about abortion on demand. More likely, he wanted the votes of people who had such concerns.

For me, working for a Democratic congressman who led a bipartisan pro-life caucus, it was increasingly clear that the Democratic Party was becoming a very lonely place for pro-lifers. Driving that point home was the fact that two other Democrats running for the presidential nomination—Senator Bob Kerrey of Nebraska and Senator Tom Harkin of Iowa—claimed to oppose abortion "personally" but refused to support any limitations on *Roe v. Wade* or abortion funding. In 1982 in the *New York Times*, Kerrey wrote that he believed "the unborn to be human life and entitled to all the protections the state can legally offer for the preservation of life." By 1992, he was pledging to appoint Supreme Court justices who would uphold *Roe*. (Clinton's ultimate choice for vice president, former Tennessee senator Al Gore, also abandoned his opposition to abortion and abortion funding, despite the fact that he once wrote, "It is my deep personal conviction that abortion is wrong.")

What propelled this about-face among so many in the Democratic Party who sought national office? It was hard to escape the fact a well-organized and generously funded woman-led movement that had defined abortion as the sine qua non of feminism was largely responsible. EMILY's List, the proabortion political action committee, raised $1.5 million in 1990; that funding helped elect two women governors in Texas and Oregon and three women to the House of Representatives, bringing the total number of Democratic women in the House to twenty (compared to nine women Republicans, many of them proabortion). By the fall of 1991, they were actively recruiting women for dozens of races around the country and well on their way to raising more than $10 million for the 1992 campaign.

In January 1992, the Supreme Court agreed to hear a challenge to the 1989 law enacted in Pennsylvania in the wake of its previous decision in *Webster v. Reproductive Health Services*. The abortion industry challenged the law immediately, but the Third Circuit Court of Appeals upheld it with the exception of the requirement for spousal notification. Planned Parenthood appealed that decision to the Supreme Court.

That same month, Governor Casey went to the National Press Club in Washington, DC, to lay out a case for the law and for the right to life of the unborn. *Washington Post* columnist Colman McCarthy characterized the speech as follows: "With as much candor as courage, Gov. Robert P. Casey of Pennsylvania has confronted fellow Democrats publicly with a truth that many of them are squirmy about privately: the party's ideological insistence that national candidates stick to one line on abortion. It is the all-or-nothing line of the National Abortion Rights Action League (NARAL), single-agenda advocates to whose recent banquet five Democratic presidential candidates piously trooped to renew their vows of abortion-rights obedience."

In April 1992, just days before oral arguments at the Supreme Court in *Planned Parenthood v. Casey*, the governor headed to Notre Dame University Law School to make his case. He said party leaders had turned Democrats into "the party of abortion" but were turning their backs on "millions of pro-life Democrats just like [him]." He argued, "When it comes down to electing a president, values and character are what make all the difference in the world. . . . I strongly believe that more than any other issue, it is abortion that defines values in American politics today."

Casey's speech was a direct rebuke to former New York governor Mario Cuomo, who went to Notre Dame in 1984 to argue that although he believed abortion to be the taking of a human life, he was not morally obligated to take any legal steps to end it and in fact was justified in supporting laws to enable and extend it, including federal and state funding. Cuomo's argument was facile and tortured (and widely ridiculed), but it gave ideological cover to a generation of Democrats who wanted to be "personally opposed" to abortion without doing anything to stop it.

The atmosphere surrounding the oral arguments on April 22 reflected the gravity of the issue at hand. *Planned Parenthood v. Casey* was the best opportunity since 1973 to overturn *Roe v. Wade*. Five of the nine justices had been appointed by pro-life presidents Reagan and Bush. Chief Justice William Rehnquist and Justice Byron White had dissented from *Roe* when it was initially decided. That the decision would come in the midst of a presidential election heightened the intensity on both sides.

As the country awaited the court's decision in *Casey*, Marty and I were anticipating a momentous change of our own. Our first child was due in May 1992. I planned to stay home after our baby's birth. But I couldn't imagine sitting on the sidelines while issues as fundamental as the right to life for the unborn were at stake. I saw staying involved in the pro-life cause as an extension of my motherhood—a way to teach my children that their lives and all other lives are precious and worthy of respect and that we must fight for what we believe is true.

Once again, I found myself thinking about what was missing—What hole in the movement was there that I could fill? The answer was staring me in the face every day on the Hill: the voices of pro-life women legislators to counter the dozens of congresswomen who spoke with authority and vigor in defense of abortion.

Before I left the Hill, I met with colleagues in politics and in the pro-life movement to gauge whether there was any support for a political effort to elect women to public office who would speak out on behalf of the unborn. The response I got was almost universally negative. Mike Pauley of the National Republican Congressional Committee—himself a stalwart pro-lifer—told me that as much as he loved the idea, his read of the party was that it would not fly. Many people, even those who were committed to the pro-life cause, said it would be virtually impossible to find pro-life women who could run and win races in the Republican Party. The "intelligentsia" of the party had decided that abortion was a losing issue at the ballot box and that the only way to attract women voters was to speak about it as little as possible. In fact, some prominent Republicans had decided to counter EMILY's List not by supporting pro-life candidates but by forming the WISH (Women in the Senate and House) List to elect proabortion Republican women. Even those who thought the idea had merit doubted that any serious money could be raised for pro-life women candidates.

I repeatedly was told that polling "proved" suburban women would abandon the Republican Party "in droves" if abortion on demand were overturned. That conclusion was based on fear more than fact; Gallup found in January 1992 that only 31 percent of all Americans believed abortion should be legal in all circumstances. The same poll found huge majorities in favor of limits like those in the Pennsylvania law at issue in *Planned Parenthood v. Casey*. Republicans were blind—perhaps willfully so—to the truth that Governor Casey was sounding the alarms over in his own party: huge numbers of Democrats were at odds with their party leadership on the issue of abortion and might be persuaded to vote for candidates who reflected their pro-life views.

The naysayers bought into a narrative relentlessly pushed by the abortion lobby and echoed by political "experts" that being proabortion was the only way to win women's votes. That message was amplified in the elite media, who dubbed 1992 the "Year of the Woman" based on the record number of women candidates for the House and Senate in the Democratic Party. There were dozens of proabortion women candidates running in 1992, but that didn't happen by accident or spring out of the political ether. The abortion lobby was aggressively pursuing its goals; the pro-life movement had abandoned the field.

The Supreme Court ruling in June on *Casey* was a muddled mess, a deep disappointment to pro-lifers, and a "clouded victory" for the abortion lobby. The decision reaffirmed *Roe* while upholding the right of states to place limits on abortion. An article published in 2016 in *Mother Jones* cited pro-life lawyer Paul Linton's assessment that "a 'moral ambiguity' about abortion pervaded the joint opinion [by Justices Sandra Day O'Connor, David Souter, and Anthony Kennedy upholding *Roe*], as well as 'the nagging sense' that the three justices thought *Roe* had been wrongly decided but upheld it anyway." For his part, Justice Scalia wrote that the decision was "hopelessly unworkable" and "really more than one should have to bear."

The bitterness pro-lifers felt after the *Casey* decision was palpable. The destruction of Judge Robert Bork's nomination to the court in 1987 led to the appointment of Justice Anthony Kennedy. Bork's certain vote to overturn *Roe* was replaced by Kennedy's muddled thinking and incomprehensible musing that "at the heart of liberty is the right to define one's own concept of existence, of meaning, of the universe, and of the mystery of human life." President Bush's selection of Justice David Souter proved equally disappointing, despite the assurances of White House chief of staff and former New Hampshire governor John Sununu that Souter's silence on the issue of life during his career as a judge masked his true identity as a stealth pro-lifer. Souter voted to uphold *Roe*.

The Bush White House breathed a sigh of relief over the *Casey* result, happy that the election would not be dominated by abortion politics. But by then, the essential shape of the 1992 election had been set, and it did not portend well for a Bush victory. A Gallup poll released on June 11 showed Independent candidate Ross Perot, a Texas businessman, leading President Bush 39 to 31 percent, with Bill Clinton trailing at 25 percent. Perot's unconventional platform included support for abortion.

The Democrats at their convention completed their conversion to an exclusively proabortion party at the national level. Governor Robert Casey, who had been elected in 1990 in the crucial state of Pennsylvania by a margin of one million votes, was denied the opportunity to speak on the basis of his pro-life views. He published a manifesto in the *New York Times* signed by dozens of Democrats that concluded with these words:

> The rhetoric of abortion advocacy contains a truth that abortion advocates often fail to perceive. Abortion *is* a question of choice. The "choice," though, is not one faced by isolated women exercising private rights. It is a choice faced by all the citizens of this free society. And the choice we make, deliberatively and democratically, will do much to answer two questions: What kind of a people are we? What kind of a people will we be? If we abandon the principle of respect for human life by making the value of a life depend on whether someone else thinks that life is worthy or wanted, we will become one sort of people. But there is a better way. We can choose to reaffirm our respect for human life. We can choose to extend once again the mantle of protection to all members of the human family, including the unborn. We can choose to provide effective care of mothers and children. And if we make those choices, America will experience a new birth of freedom, bringing within

it a renewed spirit of community, compassion, and caring.

Casey's call to action for Democrats fell on deaf ears. In the other party, President Bush was challenged by Patrick Buchanan, who in a fiery convention speech tried to lay out a pathway to a Bush victory, one that took advantage of the fact that the Democrats had essentially exiled pro-lifers and social conservatives from their party. But President Bush was not at ease with Buchanan's confrontational rhetoric and had little stomach for culture wars. In November, Bush lost to Clinton 43 percent to 37 percent, with Perot earning nearly 19 percent of the votes cast. Clinton's landslide victory in the Electoral College, with 370 votes versus Bush's 168, cemented abortion on demand as an essential plank in the Democratic platform.

The investments made by EMILY's List in the months leading up to 1992 paid off: 11 women were nominated by major parties for the Senate and 106 were nominated for the House. Of those, four women won seats in the Senate, tripling the number of women serving in that body, while in the House, twenty-four women won races, bringing the total number of women sworn into office in 1993 to forty-seven; thirty-five were Democrats, twelve were Republicans. None of the newly elected women to the House and Senate—Republicans or Democrats—opposed *Roe v. Wade.*

The abortion lobby nearly succeeded in equating feminism with abortion. But a principled remnant of the feminist movement refused to go away quietly. In March 1992, Rachel McNair, the president of Feminists for Life, decided that a pro-life response was needed to EMILY's List and the Republican-oriented WISH List. She began organizing like-minded women in a loose coalition under the banner of the National Women's Coalition for Life (NWCL). Fourteen grassroots organizations joined in NWCL's initial statement on April 3, 1992, which said in part,

> The National Women's Coalition for Life will not remain silent while society looks away from the children and women abortion destroys. Furthermore, we will not tolerate misrepresentation by a vocal minority of women who claim to speak for us on a national level. American women deserve more.
>
> Within the National Women's Coalition is a place for all women who realize that when society's answer for families in distress and women in crisis is to encourage them to dispose of their children, something is drastically wrong. We welcome women who recognize that each of us is imperfect, and that a person's worth is not conferred on them by others, but is an inherent part of being human. We welcome women who understand the responsibilities that are a part of womanhood, and motherhood. We have a place for all women who seek real women's rights, who work to eliminate discrimination, mistreatment, and who understand that abortion only blinds

us to these real issues. And we welcome women who have become abortion's other victims.

Today, we redouble our efforts in the many services we offer to heal the wounds of abortion, and reach out in compassion to women and families in pain. We will continue to provide emotional, financial, medical, and practical support to women and families who are facing parenthood with limited resources. And we will communicate to the people of America, including our elected officials and community leaders, what we know is the truth: The answer to crisis pregnancy is to eliminate the crisis, not the child. Abortion kills.

American women did, and do, deserve better than abortion—but that message could not be heard in 1992's political environment, set as it was on the idea that the key to electing more women to public office was their embrace of legal abortion. After the election, Rachel, together with friends and collaborators including Serrin Foster, Helen Alvaré, Susan Gibbs, and Mary Krane Derr, recognized that the only way to fight a wrong idea was with the power of a better idea. In February 1993, with total funding of $2,485 contributed by the groups who made up the NWCL, they launched a political action committee named for feminist icon Susan B. Anthony. They sought to reclaim authentic feminism from those who had perverted it by equating it with abortion— so who better to choose as its model than Anthony, who in addition to leading the fight for women's suffrage had been a fierce opponent of abortion, which her newspaper, the *Revolution*, called "child murder." The PAC was headquartered in McNair's office inside a pro-life pregnancy center in Missouri. I knew its founders from my work on Capitol Hill and was honored to be asked to serve as its first executive director.

The Capitol Hill launch of Susan B. Anthony List in February 1993 raised $9,000. With my daughter Hannah by my side and son Joseph on the way, I began working with the SBA List leadership toward our goal of turning 1992's "Year of the Woman" into 1994's "Year of the Pro-life Woman." In the process, we hoped to reclaim authentic feminism from the clutches of an abortion lobby founded on the gruesome lie that a woman's happiness and progress depend on her right to destroy her own child.

CHAPTER 6

The Pro-life Movement Flexes Its Muscle

THE EARLY DAYS OF SBA List coincided with the start of Bill Clinton's presidency. Clinton ran for president on an explicitly proabortion platform that endorsed "the right of every woman to choose, consistent with *Roe v. Wade*, regardless of ability to pay, and . . . a national law to protect that right." He began to deliver on that promise on January 22, 1993, the twentieth anniversary of *Roe*. In a White House ceremony, he signed five executive orders that overturned more than a decade's worth of hard-fought pro-life victories. These included a ban on counseling for abortion at federally funded facilities, a ban on taxpayer-funded medical research using tissue from aborted babies, and President Reagan's Mexico City policy, which prohibited funding for international programs that promoted abortion as a method of family planning. In his book *A Woman in Charge*, Carl Bernstein writes that Hillary Clinton was the architect of these executive actions: Bill's pollster argued that "she was dead wrong on the timing of such a hot-button issue . . . by acting on abortion policy as one of the administration's first pieces of business, the president and, worse, Hillary would be perceived as governing from the left. . . . But Hillary regarded the prohibitions in question as a powerful symbol of Reagan-era policies, and an opportunity to declare boldly that the Clinton era had begun."

Both sides were right: the reversals signaled a new era had begun, and Clinton would, at least on the issue of life, govern from the Far Left. President Clinton may have had some misgivings about making abortion a defining issue for his administration, but Hillary had none. She intended to remake the role of First Lady as a feminist icon; abortion on demand was essential to her vision.

The feminism Hillary Clinton and her allies championed would have been anathema to early champions of women's rights. In Susan B. Anthony's newspaper, the *Revolution*, the house editorial asserted about abortion, "No matter what the motive, love of ease, or a desire to save from suffering the unborn innocent, the woman is awfully guilty who commits the deed. It will burden her conscience in life, it will burden her soul in death; but oh! Thrice guilty is he who . . . drove her to the desperation which impelled her to the crime." Victoria Woodhull, America's first female presidential candidate, reportedly said in a lecture that "every woman knows that if she were free, she would never bear an unwished-for child, nor think of murdering one before its birth." Another popular feminist lecturer, Mattie Brinkerhoff, wrote in the *Revolution*, "When a woman destroys the life of her unborn child, it is an evidence that either by education or circumstances she has been greatly wronged." These are but a few examples of an overwhelming consensus among feminist pioneers.

Anthony and her allies had an expansive vision of women's rights rooted in the universal and self-evident human rights enumerated in America's founding documents. Writing in *Boston Review*, feminist historian Vivian Gornick characterizes this generation—which included Elizabeth Cady Stanton, whose *Declaration of Sentiments*, presented at Seneca Falls in 1848, sparked the first organized women's rights and suffrage movement in the nation—as "first-wave" feminists. They were animated by the "passion and conviction" that women had been denied "what had been promised them by right of birth into a democracy." This realization that the status of women was contrary to the promise of America's founding "empowered the feminists of Stanton's generation, made them the extraordinary activists they became, and went far to explain why feminism as a liberationist movement flourished in this country as nowhere else in the Western world."

The "first-wave" feminist vision was broad, comprising full civil rights and social equality, but by the time suffrage was won in 1920, after an effort of more than sixty years, Gornick writes, "the philosophical largeness of the nineteenth-century visionaries had drained away," and the movement was "by then composed of single-issue organizers" who'd expended their energy fighting for the vote.

Among the leaders of the suffrage movement as well as the broader women's rights movement was Alice Paul, a woman of personal courage and political savvy whose aggressive tactics led President Woodrow Wilson to drop his opposition to women's suffrage, an act that paved the way for the passage of the Nineteenth Amendment in the House and Senate and its ultimate ratification by the states in 1920. Paul, like so many other pioneers of the women's movement, considered abortion the ultimate exploitation of women and refused to link her later campaign for an Equal Rights Amendment to efforts to legalize abortion.

Alice Paul, who died in 1977, considered her lifelong crusade for equal rights for women largely won when the Civil Rights Act of 1964 prohibited discrimination on the basis of sex, race, color, religion, and national origin, a goal she had long pursued. By then the women's movement she had helped lead throughout most of her life was in the process of being transformed. Historian Gornick described feminism's "second wave" as the rebirth of the feminist movement with a confluence of leaders from science, literature, history, psychology, philosophy, and politics, all focused on understanding "the insecurity behind society's need to agree that women would live a half life in order that men might gain the courage to pursue a whole one." This second wave of feminism, however, coincided with—and ultimately was hijacked by—another movement for social change: the sexual revolution. By the 1980s, the takeover was complete—and the vision of the "second wave" had been narrowed "down to single-issue organizing, the issue now being abortion."

What once was a noble quest for equal rights is now led by a corrupt special interest group pushing abortion on demand. Today's "feminists" turn a blind eye to sex-selection abortion in the United States and worldwide, a travesty that amounts to a global war on little girls who are disproportionately aborted; one recent analysis suggests that from 2014 to 2018 alone, as many as 8,400 girls are missing in America due to this lethal, discriminatory practice. Big corporate abortion gets rich on the dismemberment of aborted babies and the sale of their body parts, feeding on the misery of their mothers.

These "feminists" have never met a problem abortion could not solve. The Zika virus? Abortion. Hurricane Harvey? Abortion. The 9/11 terrorist attack? Abortion. Environmental degradation? Abortion.

In her book *Subverted: How I Helped the Sexual Revolution Hijack the Women's Movement*, journalist and former writer for *Cosmopolitan* Sue Ellen Browder describes in detail the process by which the aims of the sexual revolution displaced the goals of the movement for women's rights. Browder was attracted to the National Organization for Women (NOW) in the 1960s to right the injustices women faced in the workplace—like the one she had endured when she was fired from a job because she was pregnant. She didn't know that women's equality was in the process of being redefined. As Lawrence Lader, founder of NARAL, wrote in his 1966 book *Abortion*, "The complete legalization of abortion is the *one* just and inevitable answer to the quest for feminine freedom" (emphasis added).

How did the movement that worked for so long to attain for women equal rights and opportunities come to subordinate all its goals to a quest for something the movement's foremothers considered to be the very essence of male domination, the ultimate exploitation of them? Browder's book presents a fascinating "fly-on-the-wall" look at the "room where it happened," to steal from Aaron Burr's lament from the hit musical *Hamilton*.

On November 18, 1967, about one hundred members of NOW met at the Washington, DC, Mayflower Hotel in its opulent Chinese Room for their second annual conference. Their main agenda item was the adoption of a "Bill of Rights for Women" that would serve as a blueprint for their growing movement. Among the uncontroversial issues were equal pay for equal work and government-funded child care centers. An Equal Rights Amendment to the Constitution was endorsed. And then, in the final act of the day, NOW's leader, Betty Friedan, put forth a resolution calling for the repeal of all laws against abortion. Her surprise move, in Browder's account, sparked "bitter, strident controversy"—but after hours of debate and counterproposals, Friedan's original proposal passed by a vote of fifty-seven to fourteen. Abortion was the news coming out of this conference, not equal pay or child care. One advocate of the plank told the *Washington Post* that "the abortion stand seeks to free women really from their own notions of themselves as 'slaves' to their reproductive processes." By the vote of a mere fifty-seven women, "the women's movement and the sexual revolution became united as one in the eyes of the media and the world."

As Browder writes, "On that tragic night, in the paltriness of an earthly moment, the women's movement was sharply scissored into two irreconcilable factions: women for legal abortion on demand, and women who opposed it. In the hours before midnight on November 18, 1967, NOW simultaneously became both the national organization *for* women and the national organization *against* motherhood, a living contradiction."

Twenty-five years later, when SBA List was founded, the number of women in public life who defied that contradiction and continued to be for *both* women and motherhood had dwindled. Our first challenge was to identify viable pro-life women candidates. Our second was to find donors who could contribute enough money to make a difference in their campaigns. Both were daunting.

The *Wall Street Journal* published a front-page article on October 17, 1994, that offered a snapshot of what we were up against on the fund-raising front. The article was titled "Power of the Purse: Women Are Becoming Big Spenders in Politics and on Social Causes—Feminism Is a Beneficiary; So, Too, Are the GOP and Pro-life Movement—Susan B. Anthony vs. Emily" and was a great boon because it gave us our first national publicity and placed us on par with EMILY's List. It began, "The 'Year of the Woman' was 1992, but this is the era of the woman's checkbook." The numbers the article cited made clear just how many more checkbooks were being opened on the proabortion side: against the $70,000 raised for candidates endorsed by Susan B. Anthony List in the 1993–94 election cycle stood the nearly $6 million raised by EMILY's List—"more money than the PACs affiliated with the American Medical Association, the National Rifle Association or the National Association of Realtors, long the kings of the fund-raising hill."

The *Wall Street Journal* described one of our fund-raising events that year as follows: "At Head's Great American Restaurant on Capitol Hill, scores of women crowd into a room decorated with red, white and blue balloons to discuss abortion and come across with campaign contributions for female congressional candidates who have simpatico views. But the aim of the fund-raiser isn't what some people might expect. The event, co-sponsored by . . . the Susan B. Anthony List, is to funnel money to candidates who call themselves 'pro-life.' Tonight and otherwise, the new group has raised more than $70,000 from a donor base it says is 75% women."

That event was designed to raise money for the fifteen women candidates SBA List endorsed for the House by combining small contributions from many different donors together to make a larger donation. Bundling was a way for small donors to have a big impact.

The process we undertook over that first election cycle to identify candidates worthy of support exposed some of the tensions inherent in the founding of a pro-life women's organization. We sought out women from both parties who would commit to voting for pro-life legislation. Key members of our board wanted to endorse only candidates who also supported other parts of the feminist agenda—for example, federally funded child care. More than twenty years after *Roe* and twenty-seven years after that fateful meeting of NOW at the Mayflower Hotel, those women were few and far between. The "living contradiction" built into the founding of the modern women's movement continued to bear its poison fruit, a fact that seriously compromised our ability to find candidates we could support.

Yet we did find fifteen women, both Democrats and Republicans, who met our criteria. On election night, eight of our fifteen endorsed candidates won their races, a victory rate of 53 percent, higher than that achieved by EMILY's List in 1992. Of the ten women elected to the House of Representatives for the first time in 1994, seven were pro-life; all were endorsed by SBA List. They were Enid Waldholtz (R-UT), Andrea Seastrand (R-CA), Linda Smith (R-WA), Helen Chenoweth (R-ID), Sue Kelly (R-NY), Barbara Cubin (R-WY), and Sue Myrick (R-NC).

SBA List's first election cycle proved our analysis was correct: the thing missing from the pro-life movement was pro-life women in public office. Like the protagonist in the film *Field of Dreams*, we built it, and they came. But the tensions below the surface about our overarching mission continued to simmer. Was SBA List a pro-life organization or a women's group? SBA List's leadership—and I as executive director—sincerely wanted it to be both. But as we struggled with the criteria for giving our support, one question kept coming up: Was being pro-life enough?

For me, ultimately, the answer is a simple yes. No other issue, however worthy, carries a moral weight equal to that of the unborn child in the womb. Whether our nation protects the right to life is a question of human rights, not women's rights, and the answer goes to the very heart of our founding principles. The same quest for "universal and self-evident" human rights that prompted our founders to pledge their lives and sacred honor, inspired Susan B. Anthony and others to work to extend the democratic franchise to women, and led to a bloody civil war to eradicate slavery and a civil rights movement to remove any legal protection for discrimination is what animates the pro-life movement today. There is no right more fundamental than the right to life and no way our nation can fulfill its promise as long as that right is set aside in favor of a women's right to "choose" death for her unborn child.

Our internal debate continued into 1995, but the untenable task of trying to pursue two contradictory goals ultimately led to a realignment. I became SBA List's president, supported by a board of directors that included two of the original founders. The fund-raising challenge we faced was huge; we barely had enough money to buy postage to send out fund-raising requests. But I now had the freedom to build the organization in a way I hoped would lay a foundation for future growth, which included moving SBA List into a professional office and hiring a staff. I started imploring my friends and acquaintances and any sympathetic people I met on the street to host house parties to recruit members and raise funds for SBA List. Plenty of people learned to turn and run the other way when they saw me coming.

Our first fund-raising breakthrough came with the help of Kathleen and Quinton McManus. Knowing they were generous supporters of pro-life causes, I went to them and made my case that SBA List was worthy of their time and treasure. A woman of profound faith, Kathleen immediately saw that by electing pro-life women to office we could do so much more to push back against the abortion-centric feminism that dominated and degraded political discourse. Kathleen offered to host "high tea" at her spectacular home in McLean, Virginia. Working with Kathleen and Jennifer Bingham, an experienced political hand who I hired (after many months of volunteer service) as SBA List's executive director, I set out to build a host committee for the event. Our efforts in the 1994 election cycle had been noticed on Capitol Hill; most of the congresswomen we helped elect in 1994 agreed to attend as honored guests. We developed a stealthy asset in the wives of current and former pro-life male politicians, who were savvy political operators in their own right. Among the "honored guest hostesses" we recruited for the tea were Susan Baker, wife of former secretary of state Jim Baker; Joanne Kemp, wife of former congressman and Housing and Urban Development (HUD) secretary Jack Kemp; and congressional wives Marcia Coats, Mary Bunning, Christine DeLay, Linda Nickles, Marie Smith, and Carolyn Wolf. Major benefactors in addition to the McManuses included Mary Ellen Bork, Scott and Carol McNamara, John and Barbara Quarles, Patti and Bob Schmidt, Dan and Jenny Sullivan, and Louisiana congressman Bob Livingston.

Before joining SBA List, Jennifer Bingham had worked on Oliver North's 1994 Senate campaign in Virginia. She was politically astute and well connected. Her professional network included staffers for Michigan senator Spence Abraham. Through that connection, Susan invited Spence's wife, Jane, an accomplished political organizer, to come to the tea. The tea was an enormous success—SBA List's most successful fund-raising event since its founding—and one of its most fortuitous benefits was that I met Jane. I knew right away she had the experience and skill we needed, so I began to call upon her as an unofficial advisor as often as I could.

The 1996 election cycle, coupled as it was with Clinton's reelection campaign against Senator Bob Dole, did not yield for SBA List the same results as 1994. Clinton in late 1995 vetoed legislation that passed the House and Senate to ban partial-birth abortion. His actions made him the most proabortion president in history. We raised a total of $262,000, but in the context of a landslide victory for Clinton, only two of our endorsed candidates prevailed.

It was clear to me and to SBA List's board that our endorsed candidates needed help getting their message heard in a hostile media environment. In early 1997, I asked Jane to meet me at SBA List's office in Old Town Alexandria. I intended to ask her to design SBA List's candidate training program; she had experience running similar programs for the Republican National Committee (RNC). But by the time Jane arrived at the office, I had decided to ask her to take over as SBA List's president instead while I assumed the role of chairman of the board. Marty and I had our third child in July 1996, and with three children under the age of five, I was drowning. Jane threw me a lifeline, and we launched a partnership that would help expand SBA List's reach and propel our future growth.

CHAPTER 7

Flipping the Script

The Fight to Ban Partial-Birth Abortion

WITH JANE ABRAHAM AS president and Jennifer Bingham as executive director, SBA List began to build
on the foundation of our early success. Jennifer helped
professionalize the organization and put in place the
institutional infrastructure we needed to grow. Jane was
an accomplished executive and a polished spokeswoman
whose broad experience and deep connections in her home
state of Michigan and in Congress—where her husband,
Spence, was a senator—boosted SBA List's credibility and
influence. Another important element of our success was
the political knowledge and respect that our board member Susan Hirschmann exercised on our behalf. Susan was
my old College Republican ally, all-Southern household
roommate, and trusted political advice giver, and she was
and remains indispensable to success.

One of the most important structural changes we made
was to incorporate as a 501(c)(4) in addition to being a
political action committee. With this came a new ability
to carry out independent expenditures on behalf of our
endorsed candidates as well as contribute directly to their
campaigns.

Another major change came only after serious—and
sometimes contentious—debate among our board members

and others who were intimately connected to SBA List's mission. We were founded to help elect pro-life women candidates to Congress and other offices and to demonstrate that authentic feminism embraced the rights of women and their unborn children. The women we helped elect to office proved to be effective spokeswomen for our cause. But electing women to Congress was not an end itself; rather, it was a means to a greater goal of ending abortion. Jane recognized we needed to be on defense as well as offense, and I agreed. We were just spinning our wheels if while we were electing pro-life women, the abortion lobby was defeating pro-life men. Some on our board worried "mission creep" would diffuse our resources and hamper our effectiveness; others believed we were betraying our feminist roots. But ultimately, we decided to endorse pro-life male candidates who were running against proabortion women and actively work to defeat their opponents. This move was a critical step toward SBA List adopting a more strategic approach to achieving our ultimate goal of protecting women and children from the violence of abortion.

As we expanded our work with candidates, both men and women, they increasingly turned to us for help in communicating their pro-life views in an aggressively hostile media environment. We started to run campaign schools for candidates and their staffs, based on the model developed by Morton Blackwell's Leadership Institute and with his help and encouragement. Carlyle Gregory, a Virginia-based political consultant with vast experience in winning campaigns, developed a soup-to-nuts curriculum. The Republican National Committee and its counterparts, the National Republican Congressional Committee and National Republican Senatorial Committee, spent millions each year to train candidates on issues, campaign management, and tactics. But they failed to prepare them to deal effectively and positively with the hottest of hot-button issues. Our efforts helped fill the gap; the question was, Why did we have to?

The answer was dispiriting. The Republican leadership at that time didn't train candidates on how to talk about abortion because they didn't want them to talk about it at all. Oh, they recognized the necessity of mobilizing pro-lifers to volunteer and vote, but they believed it should be done under the radar and out of the public eye. They effectively prohibited candidates from using the issue in advertising that wasn't targeted to a religious audience. This advice wasn't based on extensive polling, focus groups, or deep data analytics. Rather, it was founded on a gut instinct seemingly shared by the entire party establishment (mostly men) that women—including some of the wives of the party's biggest donors—wouldn't like it.

This indefensible conclusion made it possible for candidates who supported abortion on demand up to birth; opposed parental notification for minors seeking abortions; and favored sex-selection abortions, human cloning, federal funding of abortion, and a host of other deeply unpopular positions far out of sync with the majority of American voters to paint pro-lifers as "extremists."

In the mid-1990s, this began to change. Douglas Johnson, the longtime head of congressional affairs for the National Right to Life Committee, developed a legislative initiative to ban the most horrific of all abortion techniques—partial-birth abortion. This method, used in abortions at five months of pregnancy or later, involves delivering a living child feet-first except for its head and then killing it by puncturing the baby's skull and sucking out its brain until the skull collapses, at which point the dead child is delivered.

Banning partial-birth abortions was a worthy goal in itself, albeit one with an unlikely chance of enactment during the Clinton years. But it was also an effective way to illustrate the lengths to which the abortion lobby and its allies in Congress would go to defend unfettered abortion on demand. The debate over partial-birth abortion flipped the script by unmasking the extremes contained in a lawmaker's endorsement of a woman's right to "choose."

A bill banning partial-birth abortion was first introduced in the House of Representatives on June 14, 1995, by Republican congressman Charles Canady of Florida, with seven SBA List–endorsed women members as cosponsors, and in the Senate two days later by Republican senator Bob Smith of New Hampshire. In November of that year, after a passionate debate on the House floor, the bill passed by a vote of 288–139, with 73 Democrats joining 215 Republicans in favor. The bill passed the Senate in March of 1996 on a similarly bipartisan vote, setting up a showdown with the Clinton White House during his reelection campaign. Clinton vetoed the bill on April 7, 1996.

Clinton's support for partial-birth abortion exposed his extremism, and he knew it. His veto message conceded that partial-birth abortion "seemed inhumane" and said he would have signed the ban had it included an exception in cases where a woman's health was at risk from carrying her baby to term—an expansive loophole that would have rendered the entire ban meaningless, as numerous experts including the American Medical Association, the proabortion American College of Obstetricians and Gynecologists (ACOG), U.S. surgeon general C. Everett Koop, and even one prominent late-term abortionist stated they could conceive of no case in which this brutal procedure would be medically necessary. At a May appearance in Milwaukee, Wisconsin, alongside German chancellor Helmut Kohl, Clinton railed against the bind he had been put in by being forced to veto the partial-birth abortion ban. The *Los Angeles Times* reported that Clinton, "his voice shaking, his face flushed with anger, and his fingers jabbing the air for emphasis," erupted "in a sudden outburst that brought the presidential campaign to an unseasonably early boiling point . . . [and] angrily defended his veto of a ban to partial-birth abortions." Speaking of his putative Republican opponent, Senator Bob Dole of Kansas,

Clinton said, "I fail to see why his moral position is superior to the one I took."

Clinton's defensive posture should have alerted Senator Dole that this issue was one on which the Democrats felt vulnerable. Dole did respond that day during a speech to Catholic journalists, saying Clinton's veto had "pushed the limits of decency too far," on an issue where "nearly all Americans can come together." But "Dole actually gave the partial-birth abortion issue relatively low billing" that day, according to the *Los Angeles Times*, a practice he would continue throughout the campaign.

It's ironic that Dole would fail to take advantage of an obvious opening provided by his opponent on the issue. His first Senate reelection campaign—in Kansas in 1974—was "the race that introduced the [abortion] issue to national politics" and demonstrated "the power of abortion as a political issue," according to the *New York Times*. Dole's opponent that year was Dr. William Roy, a Democratic congressman who ran an aggressive campaign attacking Dole for his ties to disgraced president Richard Nixon. Roy was also an obstetrician who performed abortions and a supporter of *Roe v. Wade*. Dole made Roy's abortion record an issue and won a very narrow victory after carrying predominantly Catholic (and Democratic) precincts in Roy's congressional district. The *Times* reported that "Roy and his supporters have always maintained that the abortion advertisements and last-minute leaflets made the difference."

Despite a "basically perfect" pro-life voting record in the Senate in the more than twenty years since his 1974 reelection, Dole in his 1996 presidential campaign was "doing everything possible to distance himself from the uncompromising views of the most vocal anti-abortion advocates." Early in the primary season, Dole indicated he no longer supported a constitutional amendment to ban abortion, only to reverse course after a furious backlash. He hinted that he might choose a proabortion running mate (he eventually chose a pro-life stalwart, former congressman and HUD secretary Jack Kemp). In June 1996, he nearly prompted the resignation of the chairman of the Republican Platform Committee, Congressman Henry Hyde of Illinois, by saying he wanted to change the party's long-standing plank against abortion to inject a "declaration of tolerance" that would signal a softening of the party's stand on the life issue.

The party platform eventually included an eloquent passage that read,

> Faithful to the "self-evident" truths enshrined in the Declaration of Independence, we assert the sanctity of human life and affirm that the unborn child has a fundamental individual right to life which cannot be infringed. We support a human life amendment to the Constitution and endorse legislation to make clear that the Fourteenth Amendment's protections apply to unborn children. We oppose using public

revenues to promote or perform abortion and will not fund organizations which advocate it. At its core abortion is a fundamental assault on the sanctity of innocent human life. Women deserve better than abortion.

But as reported by the *Chicago Tribune*, the Dole campaign "squelched talk of [abortion] during the GOP convention in San Diego" and selected a keynote speaker—Congresswoman Susan Molinari of New York—who at the time supported abortion. Convinced that his victory depended on winning the votes of women who were disgusted by President Clinton's sexual escapades and lies and further convinced that the majority of those women were proabortion, Dole "treated the [abortion] issue like the plague" and did not "utter the 'a' word on the campaign trail" until early September, when he said he supported a partial-birth abortion ban during an appearance at the University of Scranton, a Catholic institution.

The House and Senate scheduled votes in September to override Clinton's April veto. The House easily cleared the threshold needed to override, by a vote of 285–137; the Senate vote on September 26 of 58–40 fell short of the two-thirds needed. But the fact that twelve Democrats—including Senators Joe Biden, Harry Reid, Pat Leahy, and Sam Nunn—voted to override in the midst of a national election should have set off alarm bells in the Dole campaign. A September 17, 1996, memo from Democratic pollster Celinda Lake to her clients under-scored the potency of the issue. She cautioned those who voted in favor of partial-birth abortion to "remember that no matter what we say, we cannot make voters think that late-term abortion is a good thing" and warned them that the majority of Americans who say they are pro-choice don't "view abortion as a positive choice" and "are comfortable with many types of regulation, including substantial restrictions on abortion after the first trimester." But rather than adjust his tactics to take advantage of the popularity of the partial-birth abortion ban, Dole continued to downplay the issue, refusing to bring it up during his nationally televised debates with Clinton. When his running mate, Jack Kemp, was asked about it in his debate with Vice President Al Gore, Kemp's response was so weak that Michigan governor John Engler characterized it as "almost apologetic." *Washington Post* columnist Mary McGrory opined, "The obvious reason why partial-birth abortion faded as a wedge question that could have separated Clinton from Catholic voters is that Dole chose not to bring it up." Dole lost the election in a landslide after leaving one of his most potent issues on the sidelines.

Dole's decision not to campaign as a strong opponent of abortion trickled down to the tactics of those who ran for the House. Political analyst Charles Cook noted that the partial-birth abortion issue was "not widely used in the 1996 elections" but was "extremely potent" when it was, nearly costing Senator Tom Harkin of Iowa his seat, as he "saw a comfortable lead evaporate in a matter of days" under attack on the issue from challenger Jim Ross Lightfoot. As *Roll Call* reported, this issue forced the race for Louisiana's open seat to a recount, costing Democrat Mary Landrieu "four to five points" and giving her the narrowest margin of victory in a Senate race in Louisiana history.

The Partial-Birth Abortion Ban Act was reintroduced in 1997. Once again it passed both House and Senate by comfortable margins. President Clinton again vetoed the bill, and the attempt to override failed in the Senate by a mere three votes (sixty-four to thirty-six, with sixty-seven needed to override) on September 18, 1998. Thirteen Democrats joined fifty-one Republicans in favor of the override, including Senate minority leader Tom Daschle, future Democratic leader Harry Reid, future vice president Joe Biden, and, tellingly, Senator Mary Landrieu.

Once again, Republican Party leaders and the consultant class urged candidates in the 1998 elections for the House and Senate to only mention the issue in front of carefully targeted, friendly audiences. In one high-profile race, a candidate defied this advice. Congressman Mark Neumann, a two-term congressman, challenged incumbent Democratic senator Russ Feingold of Wisconsin, who was running for reelection. Feingold was heavily favored to win and led Neumann in a poll at the end of August by a margin of 54 to 30 percent. But Neumann quickly began to close the gap in part due to his use of

Feingold's vote against a partial-birth abortion ban in his campaign materials and advertisements. In one ad, "set in a nursery with a lullaby in the background," Neumann says, "In a ninth-month partial birth abortion, the baby is delivered feet first, up to the head. The delivery is halted. And the young child's life is ended. Senator Feingold voted to keep partial-birth abortions legal. You see, it's not about Republicans or Democrats—it's about doing what's right for America." Polls showed a surge of support toward Neumann, powered by pro-lifers; by late October, the race was too close to call. Feingold won by a slim margin, but the point had been made: the pro-life issue was one that could move votes, not simply turn out already committed voters.

Was anybody listening? SBA List was largely on the sidelines as these events unfolded. We did not have the resources to get involved in national elections like Clinton versus Dole, nor did we have a lobbying arm to help deliver votes on Capitol Hill. Our focus was on identifying (mostly House) candidates, helping them succeed, and building a foundation for future growth. But we were watching carefully and learning a great deal about how to win—and lose—elections. Mark Neumann's race in Wisconsin was a test case, an "Exhibit A" that demonstrated how a smart and savvy candidate could, by exposing the extremism of the proabortion side, win voters to his cause. The polling from his race backed up this conclusion. Our challenge now was to overcome the institutional barriers that prevented candidates from taking full advantage of the issue.

I often wonder what would have happened if Republicans had decided to make limits on abortion a central part of their governing agenda in the late 1990s. We nearly overrode a presidential veto of the partial-birth abortion ban with the support of dozens of Democrats, including the party's top congressional leaders and presidential hopefuls. Would better leadership at the national level by Republicans have been able to win the three votes necessary to reach the two-thirds threshold to override Clinton's veto? But such leadership was scarce. House Speaker Newt Gingrich's *Contract with America* didn't mention the issue of abortion, and neither did the Heritage Foundation's conservative policy blueprint, the *Mandate for Leadership*.

Where was the evidence that being silent on the abortion issue won elections or that being pro-life cost candidates votes? Frankly, party leaders did not even look. Other issues were polled extensively and the cross tabs closely analyzed to determine how and why they moved voters. But on the abortion issue, there was no search for evidence. Misguided emotion and faulty instinct rendered the abortion issue off-limits. Even the pro-life movement, which heroically kept the issue alive in politics and culture against a relentless proabortion onslaught, continually fell victim at times to this defeatist attitude and acquiesced to operating under the radar.

As the 2000 presidential election approached, SBA List mobilized to support twenty-two candidates for state and federal office; we ultimately won seventeen races. We spent

$3 million in the 2000 election cycle, a pittance compared to EMILY's List, the largest PAC in the country. Jane and her husband, Senator Spence Abraham, strongly supported the candidacy of Texas governor George W. Bush. Marty and I leaned in favor of Gary Bauer, the former president of the Family Research Council and a strong pro-life conservative. Our infant daughter Teresa, born in 1999, had a cameo in one of Bauer's television ads during the Iowa caucus.

Bush prevailed in the Republican primaries and faced Vice President Al Gore in the general election. Bush's sincere pro-life views were rooted in his Christian faith; Gore was now stridently proabortion. Bush promised to sign a partial-birth abortion ban, an issue that grew in importance after June 28 when the Supreme Court struck down a Nebraska ban against "partial-birth" abortions in *Stenberg v. Carhart*, thereby invalidating similar laws in twenty-nine states. Polling done by Gallup two months before the court's decision found that 66 percent of Americans believed the procedure should be illegal; 51 percent of those favored Bush over Gore. Gallup concluded, "If partial-birth abortion does become a major issue in the 2000 campaign, then Bush would appear to be in the better position to capitalize on it politically."

But he did not capitalize on it. Bush rarely mentioned the issue of abortion in his campaign and ran no television ads that mentioned the issue. When asked in a debate about his views on abortion and the decision by

Clinton's Food and Drug Administration to allow sales of the abortion drug RU-486, Bush replied that he did not think a president had the power to overturn the decision, an odd and inaccurate answer contradicting a statement his campaign had issued earlier expressing opposition to RU-486 sales. When pressed again on the issue, Bush dodged the question, choosing instead to talk vaguely about his desire to build a culture of life.

Bush's circumspection was a deliberate strategy to downplay the issue in the general election. Bush's campaign strategist Karl Rove designed a plan in which the candidate's public statements seemed to run away from the party's base, including pro-lifers, to stake out a centrist position, while at the same time and on a tactical level, the campaign worked to maximize turnout from that same base of support.

Bush won a narrow victory after a contentious recount in Florida that went to the U.S. Supreme Court to be certified. Pro-life votes were essential to his victory. Exit polling on Election Day found that 14 percent of voters named abortion as the main issue influencing their vote; of those, 58 percent voted for the Republican and 41 percent for the Democrat, a net gain of 2.4 percent for Bush. He went on to govern as a pro-life president: he reinstated the Mexico City policy and other Reagan-era restrictions Clinton had overturned, strictly limited the use of embryonic stem cells for medical research, opposed human cloning, and signed a ban on partial-birth abortion that passed Congress in 2003. He appointed many good judges to the courts at all levels, including Supreme Court Justice Samuel Alito.

But the cynical strategy of hiding Bush's pro-life light under a bushel deprived the movement of the presidential leadership it needed—and denied it a full-fledged seat at the table where political and policy decisions are made. The consulting class *knew* how much the pro-life vote meant to Bush's victory—and yet patted us on the head and sent us to the back of the political bus. That had to change.

CHAPTER 8

The Republicans

THE GOAL FOR **SBA** List during the Bush years was to build the strength and stature we needed to ensure that pro-life votes at the ballot box translated into pro-life policy in Washington. It was an uphill battle. What we needed most were allies on the Hill who would hold their leaders accountable and make sure that when the horse trading was done, pro-lifers were not left holding the mule. We found that champion when Marilyn Musgrave was elected—with SBA List's help—to Congress in 2002 from Colorado's Fourth District.

Nearly a decade of experience as an effective state legislator had prepared Marilyn well for the "swamp" of Capitol Hill. She had a talent for bringing people together and harnessing their gifts; she soon emerged as a leader of the informal caucus of pro-life women in the House. Marilyn told me once that her goal was to get the women SBA List helped elect to compete for the title of most pro-life legislator. Her efforts helped spur women to seek out leadership roles in shepherding pro-life legislation through Congress and opportunities to speak out on the House floor. Wise, kind, and fearless, Marilyn came to Washington willing to serve those who elected her and champion the policies they believed in. For me, she was a mentor and a model of feminine leadership. From her I learned small details and large strategic insights about how to nurture and build up the role of pro-life women on the Hill.

Along with Marilyn, several other women were elected in the 2000s who would go on to become leaders of the pro-life movement. Michele Bachmann of Minnesota, Marsha Blackburn of Tennessee, Jean Schmidt of Ohio, Virginia Foxx of North Carolina, Cathy McMorris Rodgers of Washington—these are just a few of the SBA List–endorsed women elected during the Bush years who formed the core of an energized pro-life women's caucus on the Hill.

In Jane Abraham's nearly ten years as SBA List's president, she established its reputation as a serious organization and compiled an impressive record of electing pro-life candidates. Jane, together with SBA List's executive director Jennifer Bingham, created a foundation for future growth. She now wanted a role that placed fewer day-to-day demands on her time; at the same time, with our youngest son starting first grade, I wanted a more direct role in SBA List's operations and strategy. Once again, our interests aligned, and in 2006, Jane took over my role as chairman of SBA List's board of directors, and I stepped back in as president.

The main question on my mind was, How do we win? Not how do we win elections—we had proven that we could find and support successful candidates for office. But election victories were hollow unless they brought us closer to ending legal abortion. George W. Bush had been president for nearly eight years, and until the 2006 midterm election, his party controlled one or both houses of Congress. Yet the only pro-life *legislative* victory, other than the continuation of the Hyde Amendment barring federal funding of abortion, was the partial-birth abortion ban enacted in 2003. Not even a requirement that parents be notified if their daughters were transported across state lines to obtain an abortion—a law supported by 80 percent of voters or more—could get to the president's desk.

The 2008 presidential primary campaign on the Democratic side pitted Hillary Clinton against Barack Obama. Both were abysmal on the issue of life. Hillary made it clear she believed abortion on demand throughout all nine months of pregnancy was the pinnacle of "women's rights." Obama was, if possible, even worse. As an Illinois legislator, he opposed a partial-birth abortion ban and voted against a bill protecting infants born alive as the result of a botched abortion procedure. As a candidate, he said he supported abortion in part because he didn't want his daughters to be "punished" by an unwanted baby.

On the Republican side, Senator John McCain prevailed after fending off a crowded field of challengers that included former Tennessee senator Fred Thompson (whose wife, Jeri, sat on the SBA List candidate selection committee), former Arkansas governor Mike Huckabee, former Massachusetts governor Mitt Romney, and former New York City mayor Rudy Giuliani. Thompson and Huckabee had pro-life records; Romney ran as a pro-life candidate, but he and Giuliani had bad records on abortion.

McCain had a nearly 100 percent pro-life voting record in his more than twenty-five years in Congress but never made the issue a priority. In his unsuccessful 2000 presidential primary campaign, he hedged his position substantially (as did the eventual nominee, George W. Bush). Journalist Jake Tapper wrote in *Salon* that the "McCain strategy, shared by Bush, is to downplay his pro-life point of view. The message signals to pro-lifers that the candidate is committed to the cause, while pro-choicers walk away convinced that the candidate doesn't intend to do much about that fact. Both men have said that the country isn't ready for a pro-life amendment to the constitution. When asked, each declares his pro-life status and then immediately changes the subject to adoption. Neither will commit to picking a pro-life running mate or only nominating pro-life judges or Supreme Court justices." McCain broadcast a similar message in 2008.

Given this background, as the Republican convention approached, I joined with other pro-life leaders to urge McCain to choose a pro-life running mate. McCain publicly refused to commit to do so, and rumors swirled that his list included Senator Joe Lieberman of Connecticut and former Pennsylvania governor Tom Ridge, both of whom were proabortion. I never dreamed he would select Sarah Palin, the governor of Alaska. Sarah Palin embodied many of the reasons SBA List was founded and renewed genuine excitement among our team and the pro-life movement. SBA List endorsed Palin in her 2006 gubernatorial race and knew her to be an ally. But for most Republicans, she was a huge question mark.

That question was answered brilliantly in her nationally televised speech during the convention in Saint Paul, Minnesota. She electrified not only those present at the convention, including myself, but also an uncountable number of women who had been waiting for a female political leader to speak proudly of being a wife, mother, and defender of unborn life. "Sarah Palin is the whole package—she will give all Americans, born and unborn, the authentic leadership they deserve," I told the press shortly after the announcement. "There couldn't be a better vice-presidential pick. . . . Palin is a reform-minded woman who is truly in sync with the way real women think."

Those women began to mobilize at a meeting SBA List hosted at the Capitol Hill Club after the convention to launch Team Sarah, a social media effort that was up within three weeks. This website attracted over ten thousand members in twenty-four hours and ultimately grew to one hundred thousand members. Team Sarah went viral before *viral* was a common term. Everyone in SBA List's orbit wanted to unite behind Palin. As cofounder of Team Sarah, I went on Fox News to defend her against her detractors. I was speaking for a broad-based group of women who believed Palin was the political leader we had been waiting for—all of whom had only one question for her: "What can we do to help?"

As the enthusiasm for Palin kept growing, she mysteriously receded further away from her base of support.

It was only a matter of weeks before people began to be concerned about why there was no contact with Palin, no response from her. Team Sarah set up a national town hall conference call with over one million voters for her—even First Lady Laura Bush came on the call as a special guest—but Palin was a no-show.

By that time, Palin was beginning to wilt under a withering assault from elites in both parties and the media, who identified the threat "Mama Grizzly" posed and were determined to bring her down. Republicans like the pro-abortion former governor of New Jersey Christine Todd Whitman publicly criticized Palin for stepping down as governor of Alaska and for not being a viable candidate. Even McCain and his wife, Cindy, appeared to be undermining Palin, at least on the issue of life. On September 3, 2008, CBS aired an interview between Katie Couric and Cindy. Couric asserted, "Some, even Republicans, seemed surprised that Senator McCain picked a running mate who opposes abortion, even in the cases of rape and incest. . . . I'm just curious, do you agree with that?" SBA List had held an event for Cindy McCain to introduce her to pro-life activists, and I came away from it believing in the sincerity of her pro-life convictions. But in that interview, McCain indicated that she, in fact, did not agree with Palin, in an exchange that was widely reported as a breach between McCain and his running mate (and was followed up with a call to CBS News from the McCain campaign assuring them that Cindy McCain, despite saying she was "pro-life," did not actually favor overturning *Roe v. Wade*).

Under these circumstances, it is hard to imagine why the McCain campaign would agree to an interview of Sarah Palin by Katie Couric. Yet Nicolle Wallace, a McCain aide assigned to the Palin campaign and a personal friend of Couric's, arranged just such an inquisition, under ground rules no other national candidate would have accepted. The result was a prime example of "gotcha" journalism that a more experienced candidate— and a more competent staff—would have known to expect. Soon Wallace was leaking criticisms of Palin to her allies in the media to distance herself and the campaign leadership from the failure.

The onslaught against Sarah Palin made me ask aloud at the time, "What if Palin were a Democrat?" Contrast the treatment of the Democrats' first female VP nominee, Geraldine Ferraro, and the treatment of Sarah Palin. Ferraro emerged as a rock star when she ran alongside Walter Mondale in the 1984 presidential election and was strongly supported by the media in the face of questions about her family's finances. For Palin, however, it was quite a different story.

Frankly, the McCain campaign didn't know what to do with Sarah Palin or how to maximize her value to the ticket. Even though she was outdrawing McCain two to one at campaign events, the attitude after the Couric interview was to tightly script her so that she would not "mess things up" again.

But it was one aspect of Palin's personality that truly cut her off from the grassroots support and existing coalitions that were ready and willing to mobilize on the campaign's behalf. She and her most intimate advisors trusted nobody. They stonewalled SBA List's efforts, citing "legal concerns" and the idea that we were capitalizing on her name. While other groups may have been exploiting her name, we were excited and motivated to live out our mission to elect such a strong pro-life woman to national office. Her response was to remain in isolation from us and her key supporters. It was a painful and real missed opportunity.

In spite of all these disappointments, the biggest change in the role of the pro-life woman in politics was Sarah Palin. At present, few can remember the power of those early moments or how the other side was so threatened. Palin appealed to conservative women as defending her territory and rising up against danger. Initially, I could not believe it was true, that McCain had made such a good decision. What followed was ugly, and Palin, perhaps unwittingly, cooperated with the other side in diminishing her stature. Rather than being a mama grizzly who fiercely fought back against those who would marginalize and mischaracterize her, she retreated into a form of hibernation from those who could help her.

After the election, Sarah Palin agreed to speak at an SBA List breakfast in 2010. She was amiable and grateful and gave a beautiful speech, but it was an isolated event. She had the words to galvanize women to action and motivate those who had felt shut out of the political world. Palin made them feel that they finally had a voice.

Here was a woman saying the measure of your life is not your money or your career but the love you give, especially to the most vulnerable. A vice-presidential candidate who had a baby with Down syndrome and dealt beautifully with a daughter with a crisis pregnancy during the campaign was an opportunity that might come only once in a lifetime. Sarah Palin, in the end, arrived with great hope but left with great disappointment—the mystery of her flame-out still can only be partially explained by those who witnessed it.

But Palin's failure to endure as a national leader was also a product of the GOP as an institution. Republicans lacked any infrastructure to help her or mobilize her base of support. The next pro-life woman to step on to the national stage endured similar attacks. Michele Bachmann, elected to Congress in 2007, became a presidential candidate in 2011. She burst on the national scene after winning the Ames Straw Poll in 2011 with 28.6 percent over Ron Paul, Mitt Romney (the eventual nominee), Rick Santorum, and Tim Pawlenty. Bachmann was called the "Queen of the Tea Party" and made opposition to abortion an integral part of her message. Like Palin, her life, along with her husband's, embodied a positive pro-life message by providing foster care to twenty-three children in addition to raising five children of her own.

By the time the Iowa caucus was held six months later, Santorum surged to the top, with Romney a close second. Bachmann placed a weak sixth. What happened to derail Bachmann's campaign? It began, as usual, with the media. A *New York Magazine* feature article bore the title "Michele Bachmann Has the Spirit of a Psychotic Clown Serial Killer," complete with a photograph doctored to match it. This was the writer's response to what was portrayed as Bachmann's "verbal gaffe" in Waterloo, Iowa, stating that the city—her birthplace—is also the birthplace of John Wayne. She was actually referring to serial killer John Wayne Gacy, and the media mercilessly ridiculed her. Senator Barack Obama committed a number of gaffes during his 2008 presidential campaign: "I've now been in fifty-seven states—I think I have one left to go," and the mainstream media ignored this along with others within strike of an easy roasting.

After her victory at the Ames Straw Poll, Michele Bachmann was at the summit of her political power, but her treatment by *New York Magazine* set the media tone for the next six months, ranging from scorn and ridicule to deliberate neglect. Bachmann's unflinching pro-life views made her vulnerable to left-wing attacks and caused GOP leaders discomfort. The media depiction of Bachmann, exemplified in the wild-eyed *New York Magazine* picture, led to her being viewed publicly as unstable and unpredictable, a time bomb ready to explode. Despite the fact that she was a successful tax attorney and member of Congress, her fiery personality was turned into a caricature. Eventually the media rap on Bachmann began to stick, and her forceful, outspoken leadership was seen as a liability. I was disgusted by the treatment of Michele Bachmann, but unfortunately, it was no surprise.

Barack Obama defeated Hillary Clinton in the primaries and won a decisive victory in November. As disappointed as I was by the loss of the McCain-Palin ticket in 2008, I was absolutely heartbroken by the defeat of my friend and ally Marilyn Musgrave in her congressional race that year.

Marilyn was targeted by the abortion lobby in all three of her elections to Congress; they recognized the threat she posed to their agenda. In her reelection challenge in 2008, instead of recognizing Musgrave's importance as the Democratic Party did, the Republican Party withdrew its support, abandoning her in a race that could have been won. In the face of unrelenting attacks, the National Republican Campaign Committee—rather than doubling down as it should—pulled its advertising.

Musgrave was defeated by the radical left because of her leadership on life and marriage. In a shifting tactic that backhandedly betrayed an understanding of the power of those issues to move voters, her opponents attacked her with ads that focused instead on the environment, veterans, and government waste and were designed to make her look out of touch and incompetent.

The smear campaign ads produced by the gay rights group Colorado Families First, beginning with the 2004 election cycle, went beyond discrediting Marilyn Musgrave's voting record to assaulting her character. During the ad, a pink-business-suit-clad "Musgrave" is shown paying her respects to the dead by swiftly stealing an expensive watch off the wrist of the man in the casket.

All the while, the narrator of the ad explains that Marilyn Musgrave "voted to allow nursing homes to keep billing their patients, even after they're dead." Another ad starred the same Musgrave doppelgänger and falsely portrayed her as an enemy of military veterans. The constant and expansive media barrage by a broad Democratic coalition succeeded in blemishing her image. We continued to see this tactic in subsequent cycles.

SBA List devoted the resources we had on hand to Marilyn's campaign in 2008, but as election night approached, I expected the worst. I knew the nation was poised to elect a radical leftist who would do everything in his power to reverse the modest progress we had made on life during the Bush years. I grieved that the McCain campaign had deliberately sidelined the life issue and its most powerful spokeswoman, Sarah Palin. Personally, though, I knew I could handle any loss except one: Marilyn Musgrave's. As the returns trickled in, SBA List's staff and I hoped and prayed that our efforts to help Marilyn beat back the onslaught from the Left had been enough. When she lost by a substantial margin to a proabortion woman, we were devastated. I told her on the phone that night, through tears, that I wanted her to come work with SBA List to help accomplish the goals for which she had sacrificed so much. She wasn't ready to hear a "one door closes and another opens" message that night, but within a few months, she joined SBA List as vice president for government affairs and our chief representative on Capitol Hill.

CHAPTER 9

Going on Offense

A Sleeping Giant Awakes

THE OBAMA PRESIDENCY WAS as bleak as we feared. Once again, the pro-life movement was playing defense, this time against a "progressive" bent on waging a culture war from the left. Bill Clinton at least seemed to have some moral qualms about abortion; Barack Obama exhibited none.

What occupied me and the SBA List team, which now included Emily Buchanan as executive director, Frank Cannon as our chief strategist, and Marilyn Musgrave, was a simple question: How do we move from defense to offense?

An opportunity arose in 2009 when President Obama appointed longtime Republican congressman John McHugh as secretary of the Army. McHugh represented a vast district in Upstate New York that had been represented by Republicans since 1871, and he had a 100 percent pro-life voting record. A special election was called to fill his seat. Local GOP leaders, meeting in a restaurant in Potsdam, New York, chose Dede Scozzafava, a member of the New York State Assembly, to run against the Democratic Party choice Bill Owens.

Scozzafava was a poster girl for everything SBA List opposes. She sat on the board of her local Planned

Parenthood. She supported abortion on demand. When *Weekly Standard* reporter John McCormack approached her during the campaign to ask her to explain her views on abortion, she became so irate that she called the police. There was no doubt that if elected, she would have become an outspoken opponent of pro-life initiatives.

The fact that Dede Scozzafava effortlessly won the backing of the GOP establishment—including an infusion of almost $1 million from the National Republican Congressional Committee and the endorsement of prominent national leaders such as former House Speaker Newt Gingrich—perfectly illustrated the problem we faced. Would they have enthusiastically backed Scozzafava if she favored nationalized health care, called for slashing national defense spending, or wanted to gut the Second Amendment? Of course not—but the fact that she was completely at odds with the Republican platform on the issue of life mattered not a bit.

Pro-lifers weren't the only ones appalled by the party's sellout of its principles in its endorsement of Dede Scozzafava. Fiscal conservatives, too, opposed her record as a big spender in the New York State Legislature. When Doug Hoffman, a well-known, successful businessman entered the race as the Conservative Party candidate, he received an outpouring of support. The Conservative Party had long been a small but powerful player in New York politics since its candidate James L. Buckley won a Senate seat in 1971. The party was able to provide Hoffman a place on the ballot.

The Club for Growth, then led by pro-lifer Pat Toomey, now a Pennsylvania senator, spent about $1 million promoting Hoffman for his position on limited government and lower taxes. When Hoffman started receiving endorsements from the likes of former House Republican leader Dick Armey, Rush Limbaugh, Mike Huckabee, Tim Pawlenty, Glenn Beck, Sarah Palin, Michele Bachmann, and Steve Forbes, his candidacy became a real threat to the GOP's preferred choice.

SBA List, too, sensed an opportunity in this traditionally conservative Upstate New York district. We engaged for two simple reasons: First, on principle, we did not want a proabortion woman to win and become the model of what it takes to prevail in the northeast states. Second, we wanted to teach a lesson to the Republican Party about the strength of the sleeping giant that is the pro-life movement. The lesson had to be that Republicans must be pro-life in order to win—in other words, to run and lead as pro-life is the politically smart and right thing to do.

This earned us some serious flak from the GOP, who took it for granted that we would not publicly oppose a GOP nominee because Republicans overall were a "pro-life party." They didn't accept that electing a proabortion woman was contrary to our mission, regardless of party. SBA List's goal was not to be a wholly owned subsidiary of the Republican Party. Instead, we wanted to emulate the National Rifle Association—a nonpartisan group dedicated to one goal only: the constitutional rights of gun owners under the Second Amendment. (One of my proudest moments came in 2013 when Ilyse Hogue of NARAL called SBA List "the NRA of the Anti-Choice Movement.") Regardless of party, Scozzafava's election would be a massive step backward. In 2009, all seventeen Republican women in the House were pro-life; all of them were elected with SBA List's support. We were determined not to go backward.

SBA List promptly endorsed Hoffman and, with this, began our first on-the-ground grassroots campaign. In fact, in spite of all the high-profile endorsements, SBA List was the first organization on the ground, outside the campaign itself, helping the cause. We created a coalition with other groups, including the American Principles Project, Gary Bauer's American Values, and the National Organization for Marriage (Scozzafava was an early advocate for gay marriage). All the lessons we would learn from that effort coalesced into an overall pro-life election strategy to be applied to subsequent elections.

SBA List moved our staff to New York's Twenty-Third District six weeks before the election, along with an equal number of staffers from other coalition partners to mobilize voters in that district. Polls confirmed that the district's voters cared about the life issue. All across the district, SBA List staffers and I met with pro-life community leaders to recruit dozens of volunteers.

Our message to the local pro-life activists was this: "This election matters. We are here to help and to offer our ideas and resources to assist you—we can help each other." Thus we began with a real and substantial grass-roots coalition, grounded in the community where every-one worked as part of a team effort. That experience taught us a lesson we continue to employ: When SBA List goes into a district or state to engage in grassroots cam-paigning, we seek to strengthen the efforts that already exist, add resources where they do not yet exist, and leave groups far stronger than when we arrived.

One of our staffers, Natalie Valentine, a graduate of Franciscan University, reached out to all the alumni in the district knowing they would sympathize with our mission to elect Hoffman. Our team also went to abor-tion facilities and prayed with the regulars, asking them for advice and telling them about our efforts in reaching pro-life voters for Hoffman. The team noticed a full-page ad in the local newspaper supporting Hoffman and found its source, an elderly pro-life doctor in Plattsburgh who was suspicious at first, but once he met with our team, he offered his full assistance.

SBA List's team became connected to a local Catholic Church where the youth minister was a Franciscan grad-uate, but the pastor wasn't enthused by our presence or our effort. In fact, when our staff tried to put voter guides on the windshields of cars in the parish parking lot, he came out and ordered them off the property. As it turned out, the Democratic nominee, Bill Owens, was a "well-respected" member of the same parish. SBA List, in effect, was asking voters to reject the two Catholic candidates (Scozzafava and Owens) and support Doug Hoffman, a

Protestant pro-lifer who represented the teaching of the Catholic Church better than they did.

Our experience in the New York campaign confirmed for a broader audience what experienced political organizers already knew: pro-lifers have an extraordinary capacity for grassroots campaigning. People who believe that abortion is the taking of a human life are some of the most dedicated volunteers you will ever find. Other people don't have the same level of passion. Pro-lifers have already made sacrifices and waged battles in the community, the schools, even the churches. They don't mind being made uncomfortable, having stood outside of abortion clinics as people pass by expressing their displeasure. And pro-lifers have become accustomed to the kind of real characters you will inevitably meet in political campaigns. They don't get scared off. They know what they're getting themselves into.

With the help of volunteers, SBA List distributed our campaign signs and handed out literature at every polling place in the district, including church "lit drops" on Sundays. Our goal was to turn out every pro-life voter in the district for Hoffman. Our staff members organized more than 250 local volunteers to support our effort for him. We aired eight hundred radio ads during the campaign's final ten days; SBA List made thousands of get-out-the-vote (GOTV) phone calls to identified pro-life voters; distributed more than ninety thousand sample ballots; and put in place volunteers to man all the district's polling places on Election Day. Former Tennessee senator Fred

Thompson and his wife, Jeri, came to the district to campaign and brought country superstars Big and Rich.

Scozzafava saw the writing on the wall. She pulled out of the race on October 31, after polls showed Owens and Hoffman locked in a dead heat and her trailing by double digits. Did she submit to the will of the people and endorse Doug Hoffman, who had pledged to caucus with Republicans if elected? No, she endorsed her Democratic opponent. Somehow the threats and demands for party loyalty that had been so vocally expressed to us fell silent. Scozzafava cunningly timed her withdrawal to ensure her name would remain on the ballot as the Republican candidate, ensuring she would draw a small percentage of voters away from Hoffman. This strategy, devised in cahoots with the Democrats, made the difference. On the day before the election, November 2, polling put Hoffman at 41 percent and Owens at 36 percent. But with nearly 6 percent of the vote going to withdrawn candidate Scozzafava on Election Day, the final tally was 48.3 percent for Bill Owens to 46 percent for Doug Hoffman. Only 3,584 votes separated Owens and Hoffman—and 8,582 votes were wasted on Dede Scozzafava, whose name remained on the ballot.

The New York Twenty-Third Congressional District special election was a turning point for SBA List—we proved a pro-life ground game could dramatically impact an election, even in a short time. We gained a sense of what we could do if we deployed our resources on the ground— if we got out of the office and into the field. Going forward,

SBA List would be committed to putting into the field as large a grassroots effort as financial resources would allow. By the 2014 election, SBA List would be able to spend $15 million on its congressional effort.

The race was a turning point for SBA List in another way—we broke into the mainstream media when our effort was covered on the front page of the *New York Times*, which characterized the race as "a contentious referendum on the party's future, and its outcome will help shape what kinds of candidates the Republicans run as they look to rebuild their ranks in Congress next fall." Although we lost, the *New York Times* as well as other media underscored how close Hoffman had come as a Conservative Party candidate thanks to his challenge being energized by the support of pro-life and promarriage groups, especially SBA List's ground game.

In the New York race, SBA List sent a message to members of Congress that we are not going to stand aside when the GOP nominates a proabortion woman as its candidate. We are going to constantly challenge the "pro-life party" to be authentically pro-life. And we caught the attention of reenergized donors convinced of the wisdom of this approach.

A few months after the election, I wrote an op-ed that appeared on the front page of the Outlook section of the *Washington Post* under this headline: "If Republicans Keep Ignoring Abortion, They'll Lose in the Midterm Elections." I wrote, "Republicans too often treat the abortion issue like an eccentric aunt at Thanksgiving dinner—if they ignore it, maybe it will go away. . . . But year in and year out, pro-life voters consistently help carry Republican candidates into office." I predicted that if the Republicans didn't get their message right on abortion, they would suffer in the upcoming 2010 election. Citing the significant number of voters who identified both as Democrats and pro-life, I wrote, "So here's a warning for congressional Republicans: Bury our issues at your own risk."

Before it was published, I showed the op-ed to a close associate and financial supporter for SBA List who also was prominent in the Republican Party. "You need to pull it," I was told. When I did not agree, our relationship immediately and permanently changed. Party loyalty among Republicans, much like Democrats, often leads to rationalizations that result in compromising the most important of principles: the right to life and the duty to protect it.

Once the op-ed was published, I began to receive messages from friends that the GOP leaders were furious and that it was a "bad thing to alienate them." These messages came from people who substantially supported SBA List and who I believed were committed to our mission. This reaction was surprising but also clarifying. It made it easier to reaffirm that SBA List's alignment was not with any political party but only with our mission to save innocent lives. Our message to *both* parties was the same: If you really believe abortion causes the death of an innocent human being, then you have to act like it or risk the consequences at the ballot box.

CHAPTER 10

Obamacare, Betrayal, and a "Supreme" Win for Free Speech

FOR THE FIRST TIME since Bill Clinton's first term, Democrats in 2009–10 controlled both houses of Congress and the presidency. They moved quickly to capitalize on their dominance by pushing through a massive overhaul of the nation's health care system, a goal that had eluded them since the Clintons' failed effort in the early 1990s.

One priority of the Left's vision of health care "reform" was the gutting of the Hyde Amendment, which had prevented federal funding of abortion in Medicaid since the 1970s. The pro-life movement mobilized en masse to block any expansion of abortion funding in the Affordable Care Act—what had come to be known as "Obamacare." Central to that effort was the leadership of Congressman Bart Stupak, a pro-life Democrat from Michigan.

Since the death of Pennsylvania governor Bob Casey in 2000 at age sixty-eight, the Democratic Party had been without any national pro-life leadership. Bart Stupak had stepped up to fill the void, something Casey's son Bob Jr. had no intention of doing after being elected to the Senate in 2006. Stupak, together with Republican congressman Joe Pitts of Pennsylvania, sponsored an amendment that passed the House on November 7, 2009. It drew a line in the sand. The amendment forbade the federal government "to pay for any abortion or to cover any part of the costs of any health plan that includes coverage of abortion except in cases of rape, incest or danger to the life of the mother."

The White House and the Democratic leadership denied that any such funding existed in their landmark bill. In an address to a joint session of Congress, Obama claimed, "Under our plan, no federal dollars will be used to fund abortions, and federal conscience laws will remain in place." That was patently false. Under Obamacare, more than one thousand subsidized health care plans directly financed abortion (more than seven hundred still do as of 2020). Through the subsequent debate, Stupak remained firm in his insistence that abortion funding had to be removed from the bill and excluded from any further health care legislation. This was a particularly difficult position to be in, because unlike Republican (and some Democrat) pro-lifers, Stupak strongly supported the underlying health care bill.

From the beginning of Obama's term, SBA List chose to focus on the opposition to Obamacare's funding for abortion as our top legislative priority. This was in contrast with other pro-life organizations that were concentrating on defeating another Obama-endorsed initiative, FOCA, which would insert a right to abortion into positive federal law. We opposed FOCA as well, but we viewed the health care vote as an opportunity to demonstrate that the pro-life issue was potent and bipartisan. Democrats had always been a part of pro-life legislative victories, but this would be the first time the passage of a major Democratic legislative priority—the signature issue of their popular new president—was dependent upon the votes of pro-life Democrats. We made it clear that, regardless of our personal beliefs, SBA List did not publicly object to universal health care; federal funding for abortion was our *only* concern. This made it possible for SBA List to work with the House Democrats.

When I met with Congressman Stupak a few weeks before the vote, I told him how much his courage inspired me and energized the pro-life movement. We talked about the risks he was taking by resisting pressure from the White House and Democratic Party leadership to change his position. Because of his unique place in the history of the pro-life effort, I told Stupak that SBA List was going to give him the Defender of Life Award at our upcoming gala.

The three-term congressman from Michigan was grateful for our recognition and reiterated that he would not let his party affiliation determine his vote, no matter how much pressure President Obama and House leaders applied. "They know I won't fold," he told me. I told him that SBA List would be there for him, especially if it came down to a primary fight because of his vote. Our good-byes were cut short by a phone call. As the phone was handed to him, he mouthed, "Waxman" (Rep. Henry Waxman, D-CA), adding that he had been calling every other day. His coconspiratorial tone made me walk a little lighter as I left the office, but little did I know where this call was going to lead.

A few days later, the communication between SBA List and Stupak's office suddenly stopped; our persistent messages were not returned. For ten days prior to the vote, the congressman remained unresponsive. Alarmed and unsure what footing we were on, I went to his office on the day of the vote—a Sunday—to seek him out. The doors to his office were locked, and it required little effort for me to figure out what his sudden disappearance meant: unborn children had been betrayed.

As I left the Rayburn House Office Building, I sat on the steps and called Mallory at her parents' home, where her mother was making Sunday dinner. Mallory, choked with emotion, told me there was a press conference being broadcast on Fox News. She held her phone near the television so I could hear the disastrous news: Stupak and the other Democrats who were part of his coalition—with the exception of Dan Lipinski (D-IL)—had changed their votes. They caved to party pressure by accepting President Obama's Executive Order 13535, which ostensibly "guaranteed" that no federal monies would be spent for abortion procedures rather than including legislative language in the bill itself. The *Washington Post* reported later that the breakthrough had come when White House chief of staff Rahm Emanuel happened to "run into" Bart Stupak in the House gym and floated the executive order as a compromise. It was more like a fig leaf; an executive order, without the force of law, did not keep abortion funding from being part of Obamacare (as the law's subsequent implementation proved). Bart Stupak claimed he had prevailed: "I've always supported health-care reform," he told reporters, but "there was a principle that meant more to us than anything, and that was the sanctity of life." But in fact he was duped. Congressman Lipinski later told me that he had personally warned his colleagues that the executive order was a complete sham; he was ignored.

While the press conference was still going on in the Capitol, Mallory got calls from the *Wall Street Journal* and Politico trying to reach me. From the Rayburn House Office Building steps, I made the promise to a Politico reporter to defeat Stupak as well as the other nineteen defectors. One of the defectors was Congressman Mollohan, my former boss. It was one of the crushing moments of my life.

That very evening, before the final vote took place, we began to formulate a plan to defeat every Democrat who had voted for Obamacare based on the bogus guarantee of Obama's executive order. The month before the vote, we did polling in Stupak's district and the districts of ten other Democrats who at that time were holding the line against federal funding for abortion in Obamacare. We found that at least two-thirds of the voters in each district were against using tax dollars to pay for abortion. A majority of voters said they were more likely to reject a candidate who "votes for health-care legislation that includes federal government funding of abortion." We did the polling to help these Democrats fend off challenges from potential proabortion opponents; now we would have to use it to defeat them.

By the time I watched Stupak's impassioned but incoherent speech on the House floor against the Republican motion to substitute his own amendment for the entire bill, I was numb. The final vote was 219–212. Thirty-four Democrats voted with all the Republicans against Obamacare; many of them were pro-life and also opposed health care reform. Only one Democrat, Dan Lipinski, voted against a bill he would otherwise have supported because it funded abortion. Gone now was any pretense that the pro-life position was bipartisan on a national level. Bart Stupak and the nineteen other pro-life Democrats in the House provided the margin of victory for the greatest expansion of federal abortion funding in history.

The defectors tried to defend their decision to support Obamacare, but their arguments were hollow. It was clear from the outset that they had been deceived, some perhaps willingly. One of the clearest indications was that proabortion groups actively lobbied for the bill and hailed its passage, despite the executive order meant to allay pro-life concerns.

The irony was that for nearly a year, Republicans spent millions and millions of dollars to put pressure on Democrats to oppose Obamacare, but virtually none of this money was spent on Obamacare's greatest vulnerability. I had warned Republican leadership time after time that they must focus on the pro-life issues posed by Obamacare, including in the *Washington Post* Outlook article. In that era's characteristic fashion, they refused to engage on the abortion issue and missed an opportunity to defeat Obamacare. It was political malpractice.

On the night of the SBA List gala a month later, I forced myself to make a few lighthearted comments about Stupak's betrayal. In a decision to honor true leadership, I decided to give the award to our executive director, Emily Buchanan, who was at the heart of our opposition efforts to Obamacare. To this day, Stupak's award sits in her office to remind us all that votes have consequences. Governor Tim Pawlenty of Minnesota rallied the crowd, and despite our intended honoree having made himself persona non grata, the dinner was a great success, with the crowd energized and resolved to fight back.

We left the gala ready to tackle the gargantuan task ahead. We set out to defeat every one of the twenty pro-life Democrats who had betrayed the unborn by voting for Obamacare and its expansion of abortion funding. The day after the Obamacare vote, we sent press releases to each of their districts announcing our determination to ensure they lost their reelection campaigns in November 2010. We weren't alone in our outrage. Pro-life activists and donors across the nation were united in pursuing this goal.

Our message to voters was very simple: your congressman voted to approve federal funding for abortion by supporting Obamacare. We delivered our message via TV and radio ads, direct mail, billboards, and later direct campaigning, including a bus tour through the districts of some of the targeted members.

Bart Stupak would eventually announce his decision to retire, apparently aware that the polling in his district spelled the end of his congressional career. But most of the other pro-life Democrats whose votes made possible Obamacare's vast expansion of federal abortion funding moved forward with their campaigns, unwilling to believe that their vote could cost them the support of a key constituency they needed to prevail in November.

One of those who knew a vote to expand abortion funding could cost him his seat, however, was Steve Driehaus, a freshman congressman who represented Ohio's First District.

Throughout the Obamacare debate, Driehaus publicly stated that he would oppose any bill that did not bar federal funding for abortion. Just a week before the vote, on March 14, 2010, in an interview with the *Cincinnati Enquirer*, he stated he would "not bend on the principle of federal funding for abortion." When the White House later announced its executive order, Driehaus denounced it, describing it as nothing more than an accounting gimmick. The very next day, Driehaus joined Stupak and most other pro-life Democrats in voting yes.

How did Driehaus explain his flip-flop? His answer was a perfect illustration of self-deception and denial. He said, "I didn't change my vote. . . . My position has been consistent the entire time. I said I couldn't vote for the bill unless I had assurances that there would be no public funding for abortions and that was consistent the entire debate." He went on to praise the executive order.

To maintain this cognitive dissonance, Driehaus hit back hard when SBA List pointed out that his vote had, in fact, authorized federal funding of abortion through Obamacare. He took his complaint to the Ohio Election Commission (OEC) and accused SBA List of making a "false statement" in its billboard that read, "Shame on Driehaus! He voted for taxpayer funding of abortion." Driehaus's attorney sent a letter threatening to sue the owner of the billboards, Lamar Companies. Lamar chose not to put our billboards up. When we received the news that our billboards wouldn't be put up, our response was to double down.

A few weeks before the election, the OEC found probable cause that SBA List had "misrepresented" Driehaus and allowed his pleading to proceed. The Ohio branch of the American Civil Liberties Union filed an amicus brief in support of SBA List, a sign that the issues at stake went beyond the specific question of Driehaus's support for abortion funding to a more fundamental question of freedom of political speech. Ohio was one of the few states in America where a state election commission was allowed to determine the truth or falsity of election statements. Consequently, we filed a motion in federal court challenging the constitutionality of the OEC's role.

Using the probable cause ruling, Driehaus once again made the public argument that his vote for Obamacare did not sanction federal funding of abortion. "Not one dime of federal funds is being used for abortions. . . . We're not going to let the [SBA List] run around lying about our record." There was one problem with his statement: he was the one who was lying.

The day after Driehaus's attack on our veracity, we announced a $50,000 radio ad buy throughout his district. We could not let Driehaus's attack on our credibility go unchallenged. In addition to radio ads, SBA List conducted a week-long campaign bus tour that took us through several states, including Driehaus's district in Ohio and Kathy Dahlkemper's in Pennsylvania. Following Driehaus's lead, Dahlkemper accused SBA List of lying, using the OEC's finding of "probable cause" as evidence.

I liked Kathy Dahlkemper very much—and she had been a good friend to SBA List. It grieved me to have to oppose her reelection. But she continued to insist that the bill contained no funding for abortion. In response, we placed newspaper ads quoting the statement of the United States Conference of Catholic Bishops (USCCB) saying the direct opposite.

It was harder to forgive the actions of Kristen Day, president of Democrats for Life. Kristen was a trusted ally, dating back to my time on Capitol Hill. She was a key partner in our pro-life coalition to pass the Stupak-Pitts Amendment during the health care fight. I trusted her, and we were in complete agreement on the need for statutory language to protect life in the health care bill. So it struck me as bizarre when she called me one day and insisted that it was urgent we speak right away about the implications of the final health care bill on abortion. She asked a series of questions about where exactly in the bill the abortion language was located. What I didn't know was that she was searching for answers that could be used against me and SBA List in the Ohio case. She later filed an affidavit to the OEC using the conversation as evidence. In addition, that affidavit included confidential conversations from our coalition meetings that implicated other pro-life allies. This was no small matter, as the Ohio law allowed for criminal penalties that included massive fines and jail time.

But Driehaus, Dahlkemper, and Day had dual motives. They had long sought national health care reform along the lines of what Obamacare provided. They believed it was just and humane. They also opposed federal funding for abortion. When the two issues collided, they chose health care reform over life. They couldn't justify that utilitarian choice—how could they? Their only option was to pretend it had been no choice at all.

The hardest race for me personally was the effort to beat my former boss, Alan Mollohan. He taught me one of the most important lessons I ever learned in politics: "If you shoot a bear, you have to kill it." On May 11, 2010, after extensive SBA List efforts in the primary, Alan Mollohan was defeated. After Stupak, Alan Mollohan became the second pro-life Democrat to be out of a job.

On November 2, 2010, Steve Driehaus, Kathy Dahlkemper, and eleven other Democrats who betrayed their pro-life principles to vote for Obamacare lost their bids for reelection. SBA List had helped defeat them, as we had promised, but the victory was bittersweet. Their votes for Obamacare provided its margin of victory in the House. If these pro-life Democrats had held firm to their convictions and rejected the false promises of the executive order, I'm convinced President Obama and the White House leadership would have agreed to their demands rather than allow his top domestic policy priority to fail.

The 2010 election delivered a landmark gain for us—the election of Kelly Ayotte to the United States Senate. Since the departure of Elizabeth Dole from the Senate in 2008, that body had lacked any pro-life women members. As attorney general of New Hampshire, Ayotte defended a law requiring parental notification when a minor sought an abortion. The law was challenged by Planned Parenthood in a case that went to the Supreme Court. SBA List spent $150,000 in the primary campaign on Ayotte's behalf. Ayotte prevailed in a hotly contested Republican primary race against Ovide Lamontagne, a favorite of many movement conservatives. Her landslide victory in the November election over Congressman Paul Hodes gave us a foothold in the Senate. Speaking at our gala in 2011, Ayotte said "the reason" she won was the work of SBA List. She said, "Victories don't just happen; it is because of the work everyone in this room does."

Election Night 2010 was a turning point for SBA List. It was the most successful election in our history. Because of the work of so many conservative groups and our pro-life allies, a pro-life Republican majority took control of the House of Representatives. It was generally acknowledged that SBA List and the abortion issue had played a big part in this happening. Four SBA List-endorsed women won governorships, including Susana Martinez in New Mexico and Nikki Haley in South Carolina. That night, I cried tears of gratitude and relief. In the wake of the election, we received more good news. The now defeated Congressman Driehaus withdrew his complaint from the OEC, as it was now moot. But the peace of November was shattered on December 3, when he filed a civil defamation lawsuit against the SBA List, claiming damages were owed him for his "loss of livelihood" based on libel and asking for a jury trial. I was stunned by this novel gambit. No other candidate in the history of the Republic had ever made such an outlandish claim in the face of defeat at the ballot box.

The essence of Driehaus's case was that he had lost his reelection and thereby had been deprived of his "livelihood" as a direct consequence of SBA List's "false claim" that he had voted to approve abortion funding via Obamacare. There was only one catch: he *had* voted to approve abortion funding via Obamacare.

What was Driehaus's purpose in pursuing this litigation? And who was paying for it? Those questions have never been answered. But SBA List could not run away from this challenge, no matter how many millions it would cost in legal fees. Driehaus had questioned our integrity and credibility, but even more fundamentally, he had tried to prevent us from exercising our right to free speech. We responded to Driehaus's suit in January 2011, filing a brief in the U.S. District Court for the Southern District of Ohio denying the claim that we had misrepresented Driehaus's vote. We now had parallel court cases going at once. One was attacking the constitutionality of Ohio's false statement law and the other was defending against Driehaus's defamation claims.

In the challenge to the Ohio law, our argument was simple: How could such a body appropriately determine the truthfulness of political speech? Even though the commission was required to have three Republicans, three Democrats, and one Independent, all were appointed by the governor, and partisanship would inevitably color the commission's decisions. SBA List argued that just the presence of a commission tasked with this responsibility is a tacit danger to free speech.

In September 2011, we suffered setbacks in both cases in the Ohio federal district court. Judge Timothy Black, a former board member of Planned Parenthood Cincinnati and an Obama appointee to the court, found that Driehaus's defamation lawsuit could go to trial. That case was not resolved until March 6, 2015, when the Sixth Circuit Court of Appeals ruled that SBA List did not defame Congressman Driehaus in the 2010 election.

Judge Black in 2011 also dismissed our challenge to the Ohio "false statement" law, saying we lacked standing because the OEC had never ruled and the election was over. SBA List then turned to the Sixth Circuit Court of Appeals, which rejected our effort to overturn the Ohio law on similar grounds. Our last hope was a slim one. We asked the U.S. Supreme Court to grant cert in the case. Only a tiny fraction of such requests are granted, and an even tinier fraction of cases are accepted on a standing case rather than a merits case. Improbably, the Supreme Court granted cert. In our brief filed with the court on February 24, 2014, we argued, "In this case, application of the Sixth Circuit's restrictive rulings has assured perpetuation of a blatantly unlawful regime under which bureaucrats are the supreme fact-checkers for every political campaign—a regime that has, predictably, been routinely abused and will continue to be, absent this Court's intervention."

The Supreme Court decision was unanimous in our favor. The court's opinion, written by Justice Clarence Thomas, focused on the law's practical impact. The "false statement" law created a substantial disruption in the climate of political campaigns, allowing one candidate to gain an advantage over another: "The target of a false statement complaint may be forced to divert significant time and resources to hire legal counsel and respond to discovery requests in the crucial days leading up to an election." Always hostile to the pro-life message, the media reacted predictably. The Huffington Post carried the headline "Supreme Court Moves toward Legalizing Lying in Campaigns."

With the path cleared by the Supreme Court decision, we once again challenged the constitutionality of the Ohio law in federal court in the U.S. District Court for the Southern District of Ohio. On September 11, 2014, district court judge Timothy Black reversed his position, siding with SBA List on the issue of constitutionality.

The now-chastised Judge Black, in a complete reversal, wrote in his decision, "At times, there is no clear way to determine whether a political statement is a lie or the truth. What is certain, however, is that we do not want the Government (i.e., the Ohio Elections Commission) deciding what is political truth—for fear that the Government might persecute those who criticize it. Instead, in a democracy, the voters should decide." Black's decision even quoted this statement from the SBA List oral arguments: "[We are not] arguing for a right to lie. We're arguing that we have a right not to have the truth of our political statements be judged by the Government."

In addition to massive amounts of staff time and sleepless nights, we spent $2.1 million to fight these cases. In the end, we received a partial reimbursement check from the State of Ohio, whose law was declared unconstitutional, in the amount of $1,000,000.

CHAPTER 11

A One-Sided "Truce"

OUR DECISION TO HOLD accountable the congress-men who betrayed their pro-life promises to vote for Obamacare's massive expansion of abortion funding brought SBA List into national prominence. As the 2012 election approached, we were determined to take advantage of every opportunity that prominence provided to pursue legal protection for unborn babies and their mothers.

The 2010 midterm election delivered a "shellacking" to President Obama and his party, driven largely by opposition to Obamacare. Republicans won six seats in the Senate and regained control of the House; the House saw its largest turnover in seventy years. SBA List played a major role in delivering the victory. During the 2010 election cycle, we spent $11 million in ninety races, sixty-two of which resulted in victories. In addition to defeating fifteen of the twenty formerly pro-life Democrats who voted for abortion funding in the health care reform bill and helping elect Senator Kelly Ayotte of New Hampshire, we increased the number of pro-life women in the House by 70 percent and the number of pro-life women governors from one to four.

In the election's aftermath, Congressman Eric Cantor of Virginia, a member of the House Republican leadership, said, "We've been given a second chance and a golden opportunity. . . . People want to see results." The House did move quickly to pass legislation to make the Hyde Amendment permanent and repeal Obamacare, including its expansion of abortion funding. But simmering below the surface again was the idea that Republicans should put social issues to the side in favor of a singular focus on the economy. In a wide-ranging profile published in the *Weekly Standard* in its June 14, 2010, issue, popular (and pro-life) Indiana governor Mitch Daniels, widely considered a leading contender for the 2012 Republican nomination, said Republicans "would have to call a truce on the so-called social issues. We're going to just have to agree to get along for a little while." At an event at the Heritage Foundation, Daniels was asked to clarify his position. Reporter John McCormack asked him whether he would reinstate President Reagan's Mexico City policy, which barred federal funding of abortion overseas. Daniels responded, "I don't know."

Daniels's call for a social issues truce was denounced by conservative leaders and most of the other potential presidential candidates. As my colleague Frank Cannon wrote in an op-ed published by Fox News, "Calling for a truce on social issues is a little like asking the kid being pummeled by the schoolyard bully to stand down. All the kid is doing is holding his hands in front of his face to ward off the blows." Pro-lifers were trying to restore protection for unborn life in the face of aggressive attacks from the Left; a truce was really a call for surrender. Cannon's article was titled "How to Lose the Presidential Nomination in Two Days," and in fact, Daniels ultimately decided in May 2011 not to become a candidate for the Republican nomination.

But the "truce" idea did not die with Daniels's potential candidacy. Gov. Haley Barbour of Mississippi, another potential 2012 candidate, similarly mused in September 2010 that Republican candidates should focus on the economy and issues "people care about" rather than "run down rabbit trails" on social questions. It was almost as if they did not understand who elected them to office in the first place and for what purpose.

To counter this erroneous idea, SBA List and our allies focused first on reaffirming a commitment to life from the core of the party—the Republican National Committee. On Monday, January 3, 2011, in a packed ballroom at the National Press Club, I was one of the questioners at a debate held for the candidates for the RNC chairmanship—only the second such debate in the history of the Republican Party. The fact that the debate was cosponsored by Americans for Tax Reform's Grover Norquist underscored that while party leaders might favor a "truce," the grassroots supporters of both economic and social issues did not. My role permitted me to preinterview each of the five candidates, including the incumbent, Michael Steele. I was also able to ask whether the right to life was central to the GOP's issue commitments.

The debate proved that the 2011 GOP had an unshakable core—and this core exercises real influence over the expressed convictions of the GOP's national leaders. Only two years earlier, then RNC chairman Michael Steele—who was a board member of the Republican Leadership Council—told *GQ* magazine that he believed abortion was an "individual choice." Maria Cino, one of the four leading challengers he faced, served on the board of WISH List, a political action committee devoted solely to electing proabortion Republican women. Yet at the debate and in Skype interviews SBA List conducted in advance and made public, they and the other three candidates—including the eventual victor, Reince Priebus—affirmed without hesitation their determination to support the Republican platform's social-issue stands and to carry out that support in the party's programs, from recruiting candidates to buying ads to microtargeting votes. The candidates were competing for votes from the leadership of state and territorial Republican parties, the committee men and women who are most in touch with the thinking of the GOP grassroots. The message was clear: if the leaders' pro-life convictions go this deep, the national grassroots must be overwhelmingly so.

The aura of unity sorely exasperated professional cynics like the *Washington Post*'s Dana Milbank, who fumed for his readers, "The candidates were nearly dissent-free. Abortion? All opposed. Lower taxes? All in favor. Gay marriage? All opposed. Cutting spending? All in favor." Even Jon Stewart got in on the act, lampooning the forum in a routine that vastly increased my "cool factor" with my teenage children.

Even Governor Daniels got the message. In another attempt to explain away his "truce talk," he said his message was not directed at social conservatives but at the people "aggressively trying to change the definition of marriage." His advice was meant, he said, for the liberal activists: "Stand down for a while" so the country can focus on its deepening fiscal crisis. It seemed as though a "truce" had been called on truces.

I wrote shortly after the debate, "One week into the two-year cycle that leads to the reelection or defeat of Barack Obama, the GOP truce on internal disunity is turning out to be the one that really counts." But all the progress made at the RNC could be undone, of course, by a Republican president who did not, so to speak, "get the memo." The unpopularity of Obamacare among the grassroots of both parties, coupled with a sluggish economy, created an opportunity for Republicans to make huge gains in 2012, even including the rare feat of unseating an incumbent president. Polls in 2011 consistently showed support for Obama's reelection at under 50 percent of likely voters. SBA List's top priority was to make sure all the possible Republican nominees committed themselves without exception to a pro-life agenda. The biggest obstacle to this goal was the one Republican contender who took the "truce" idea to heart: eventual party nominee, former Massachusetts governor, and now one of Utah's U.S. senators Mitt Romney.

Romney was an enigma. A devout Mormon, he set aside his faith's pro-life teachings to run as a proabortion candidate for governor of Massachusetts in 1994 and 2002, asserting that he would always "protect and preserve a woman's right to choose." His wife, Ann, made a donation to Planned Parenthood from their joint checking account at a fund-raising event they both attended. As he prepared to run for the Republican nomination in 2008, Romney let it be known that he had undergone a conversion on the issue, prompted by a conversation with Dr. Douglas Melton of Harvard's Stem Cell Institute about the horrific practice of fetal farming—creating human embryos for medical research via cloning only to destroy them. I welcome converts to the pro-life cause; I am one myself. However, some questioned whether Romney's commitment to the issue was a tactic more than a true change of heart. My view is that you take folks at their word and then help candidates become the leaders they say they are.

Questions about Romney's sincerity took on an urgency as the 2012 primary season approached. The 2012 field was crowded, but Romney had a distinct edge in fund-raising and stature. Taking a cue from the successful tax cut pledge pushed since 1986 by Americans for Tax Reform and some wise counsel from its president, Grover Norquist, SBA List developed its own pro-life pledge, and in May 2011, we unveiled it, asking every presidential primary candidate to make specific promises to defend life through legislation and judicial appointments. We asked pro-life citizens to take a similar pledge, to vote only for candidates who committed themselves to the movement's priorities. We wanted to make crystal clear what we expected in exchange for our support.

Our pledge asked candidates to commit to the following:

- only nominate to the U.S. Supreme Court and federal bench judges who are committed to restraint and who apply the original meaning of the Constitution, not legislate from the bench
- select pro-life appointees for relevant cabinet and executive branch positions, in particular the head of the National Institutes of Health, the Department of Health and Human Services, and the Department of Justice
- advance pro-life legislation to permanently end all taxpayer funding of abortion in all domestic and international spending programs and defund Planned Parenthood and all other contractors and recipients of federal funds with affiliates that perform or fund abortions
- advance and sign into law a Pain-Capable Unborn Child Protection Act to protect unborn children who are capable of feeling pain from abortion

I was disappointed but not surprised that some in the GOP leadership did not appreciate our initiative. They saw the pro-life movement as an asset to be managed, not a partner in setting the agenda. Some seemed to deal with us as if we were a remote and mysterious species to be bought off with the equivalent of the shiny beads and baubles that delivered Manhattan Island to the Dutch in 1626. When the lives of more than twenty-three hundred unborn babies are at stake each day, that's just not good enough. The votes of the pro-life movement are crucial to virtually every GOP victory in the nation. The pro-life agenda deserves to be integral to every campaign and governing agenda.

As much as Republican elites disliked our effort, the grassroots loved it in equal measure. Most of the Republican primary candidates signed the pledge without any hesitation. For Rick Santorum, Ron Paul, Michele Bachmann, Rick Perry, Tim Pawlenty, and Newt Gingrich, our pledge lined up perfectly with their own convictions. Herman Cain, after some initial concerns, signed on too. Only two candidates refused: former Nevada governor Gary Johnson and Mitt Romney.

Johnson's refusal was expected; he was a proabortion libertarian. Romney's was problematic. He characterized the pledge as having "unforeseen consequences." When asked to explain, his spokeswoman, Andrea Saul, said, "The pledge calls for legislation to strip taxpayer funding from hospitals around the country, and strictly limits the choices a President would have to appoint cabinet members." Both claims were spurious; the pledge only denied federal funding for facilities that performed or funded abortions, and the only cabinet positions constrained were those whose departments had direct responsibility for issues related to the right to life.

While I did consult with trusted pro-life ally Peter Flaherty at the campaign, I did not have a close relationship with Romney. All the campaign staff members were courteous, but it was clear their primary concern was to neutralize the pro-life issue rather than highlight and energize it. Through surrogates and allies in the media, the Romney campaign lashed out at SBA List over the pledge. I was most disappointed by conservatives who seemed to argue that since Romney might be hurt by his failure to sign the pledge, it would be better not to have a pledge at all. Less surprising was the reaction of the *Washington Post*'s "conservative" blogger Jennifer Rubin, who claimed Romney was not treated "fairly." Rubin's overwrought defenses of Romney throughout the 2012 campaign seemed to me more like those of a lovesick schoolgirl than an objective journalist.

In June 2011, Romney released his own version of a pro-life pledge. In it he stated his support for reversing *Roe v. Wade*; stopping taxpayer funding of abortion businesses like Planned Parenthood, upholding the Hyde Amendment, and reinstating the Mexico City policy; advocating for the Pain-Capable bill; and appointing constitutionalist judges. In these ways, it mirrored the SBA List pledge, but he refrained from making a specific commitment to appoint only pro-life executive branch personnel. Although the pledge repeated his objections, we were pleased that Romney had defined his specific pro-life commitments.

Romney's surprise loss to former Pennsylvania senator Rick Santorum in the Iowa caucus on January 3, 2012, should have been a wake-up call to Romney and the party leadership. Santorum was a hero to pro-life voters for his courageous efforts to pass the Partial-Birth Abortion Ban. His dogged grassroots campaign in Iowa on a shoestring budget resulted in a victory that stunned the well-financed Romney and his establishment supporters. Central to Santorum's message was his commitment to do all in his power to overturn *Roe v. Wade*, ban federal funding of abortion, and appoint pro-life judges.

SBA List had never endorsed in a Republican presidential primary and did not intend to in 2012. But Santorum's surprise victory set up the possibility of a one-on-one contest for the nomination between him and Mitt Romney, a match-up that could bring the life issue to the fore. In February 2012, right before the Michigan primary, we decided to get behind Santorum's campaign. After our endorsement, SBA List got blasted by Romney donors, the GOP establishment, and much of the conservative media. We gave Santorum substantial help, doing bus tours and paid communications and mobilizing other grassroots groups. He won the popular vote in eleven primaries in the South and Midwest but ultimately came up short. When his effort failed, the pundits were quick to blame it on his pro-life views. What they failed to notice—or deliberately overlooked—was this was the same conviction that gained him a national following and propelled him to near victory against a candidate who vastly outmatched him in organization and funding.

When Romney won the nomination and chose a pro-life Catholic, Congressman Paul Ryan, as his running mate, SBA List endorsed the ticket. At the 2012 Republican National Convention, however, it was made painfully clear that pro-lifers were on the outside looking in. The Democrats paraded proabortion leaders on their main stage and in front of the TV cameras—including the presidents of Planned Parenthood and NARAL, who spoke in prime time. At the Republican convention in Minnesota, not one pro-life leader was given a platform, and the issue itself was barely mentioned. SBA List still tried to help the Romney-Ryan ticket; whatever our misgivings, it was a vast improvement over Obama's abortion radicalism. The lack of enthusiasm from the top of the ticket nevertheless came through loud and clear to the grassroots and donors—money and volunteers dried up.

During the campaign, Romney's natural aversion to the abortion issue was bolstered by the firestorm that erupted over what came to be known as the "Akin moment." Todd Akin, a five-term congressman from Missouri, was campaigning for a Senate seat and was defending his position against abortion even in cases of rape. Mercifully, the number of pregnancies that result from this obscene violation of a woman are few (and SBA List does occasionally endorse candidates who allow for abortion in this circumstance). But those who support abortion on demand up until the moment of birth always bring up the tragic and rare possibility to deflect attention from their own extremism.

In response to this question about whether he supported abortion in cases of rape or incest, Akin said, "Well you know, people always want to try to make that as one of those things, well how do you, how do you slice this particularly tough sort of ethical question. First of all, from what I understand from doctors, that's really rare. If it's a legitimate rape, the female body has ways to try to shut that whole thing down. But let's assume that maybe that didn't work or something. I think there should be some punishment, but the punishment ought to be on the rapist and not attacking the child."

The reaction was swift and scathing. The phrase "Akin moment" has become part of the political vocabulary to describe the self-immolation of candidates when they make comments deemed unforgivable by the establishment. Romney and the GOP immediately ran from Akin, essentially ceding a winnable Senate seat to the Democrats. Akin's funding and support collapsed. For his part, Romney refused to do interviews with reporters who would ask about Akin. Along with other GOP leaders, Romney called for Akin to drop out of the race.

SBA List was one of the only organizations that did not withdraw support from Todd Akin. Did I agree with Akin's formulation? Certainly not. SBA List supported Akin's primary opponent, Sarah Steelman, because we believed she was a better spokesperson for the pro-life cause. But at this moment of crisis, we decided our responsibility was to model how we expected the GOP to behave when a candidate got into trouble on the issue of abortion. I issued a statement that read,

> Congressman Akin, a longtime pro-life leader, has said he had misspoken, and no one is arguing that rape is anything but a despicable, horrible crime. Abortion supporters like Sen. Claire McCaskill are trying to use this issue as a smokescreen to hide from their radical, pro-abortion records that are out of step with the majority of Missourians and the American people. On the issues of taxpayer funding of elective abortion in Obamacare, protection of unborn girls being targeted in the womb solely because of their gender, and whether children capable of feeling pain in the womb should be protected, President Obama and Senator McCaskill have been on the wrong side, showing that they favor abortion on-demand, for any reason, up to the moment of birth, subsidized by the taxpayers. If President Obama and Senator McCaskill care to focus on extreme positions, it is time for self-reflection. It is time to answer the question why this president has recently rejected bans on gender selection and late term abortions. Todd Akin, on the other hand, has a record of voting to protect human life. His opponent does not. Congressman Akin has been an excellent partner in the fight for the unborn.

I did not defend Akin's statement, but in that instance and others, I sought to put his gaffe in contrast to the determined extremism of the proabortion side. By then it was too late. Completely abandoned by his party, Akin lost to McCaskill, 54 percent to 39 percent. We received a lot of criticism for our continued support of Todd Akin. But if Akin's verbal blunder had been about economics or foreign policy or even gun control, what would have happened? Mitt Romney himself might well have remembered how a single word choice, by his father, George, in the 1968 presidential primary, could unfairly upend a good candidate's campaign. With the Senate on the line, Romney and the GOP leadership could have found a way to help Akin recover from his stumble.

Instead, they ran away. It was as if any mention of rape and incest acted as a Jedi mind trick on Republicans, erasing their memories and tying their tongues on the truly extreme positions their pro-"choice" opponents held. If his party had supported him, Akin could have reframed his argument to force his opponent to defend her own extremism, including support for late-term abortion, approval of sex-selection abortion, votes for federal funding of abortion, and opposition to parental notification when minors sought abortion. McCaskill's views on these issues were deeply unpopular with Missouri voters. But Romney, the RNC, congressional leadership, and many other conservatives had no idea how to intervene and help Akin and no desire to learn. One GOP leader called me in the middle of the controversy and said, "Do the country a favor and hire Todd Akin" so he would drop out of the race. The "Akin moment" became the justification for Romney not devising any effective life strategy in his campaign.

The "Mourdock moment," which came very soon after Akin's, was perhaps even worse. Richard Mourdock, who served as state treasurer in Indiana, rode the wave of Tea Party support and won the 2012 GOP nomination over six-term incumbent Senator Richard Lugar. Lugar was popular among the GOP establishment, a "wise man" on foreign policy who led Republicans on the Senate Foreign Relations Committee. While in a debate with his Democratic opponent, Congressman Joe Donnelly, Mourdock was asked about Todd Akin's comment.

Mourdock replied, "I know there are some who disagree, and I respect their point of view, but I believe that life begins at conception. The only exception I have to have an abortion is in the case of the life of the mother. I just struggled with it myself for a long time, but I came to realize: Life is that gift from God that I think even if life begins in that horrible situation of rape, that it is something that God intended to happen."

Mourdock argued that since God made every child, even one who issues from a rape or incest should be welcomed into life and not aborted. The Democrats twisted this, saying he had claimed that rape itself was preordained by God, part of "God's plan." Mourdock, like Akin, watched helplessly as the GOP distanced itself from him, fund-raising went down, and his campaign suffered a slow death. SBA List defended him, but Mourdock lost in what Politico called a "stunning upset" to Donnelly.

Both Akin and Mourdock affirmed, in Romney's mind, everything he had been predisposed to think about the abortion issue—stay far away, never plan for it, never think about it, pretend it doesn't exist. In other words, call a truce. This self-imposed ignorance was displayed in the presidential debates when Obama claimed that Planned Parenthood pays for mammograms, which in fact they don't, but Romney wasn't prepared to point out Obama's well-established false claim.

The fact is that Romney-Ryan abandoned the field on the issue of abortion. The Obama campaign ran ads in eight swing states attacking Romney for his opposition to *Roe v. Wade* and abortion funding. Planned Parenthood ran ads attacking Romney on similar grounds, with heavy buys in the swing states of Ohio and Virginia. The Romney campaign responded by running an ad that conceded the main points but pointed out that he did support abortion in cases of rape, incest, and the life of the mother. While Romney fussed over the semantics, he let Obama's extremism go unmentioned. What might have happened if instead he had run an ad saying, "You better believe I want to prevent late-term abortion and stop government funding of abortion. The question is, Why does Barack Obama support abortion in the ninth month of pregnancy, using your tax dollars to support it?"

SBA List ran a video ad that did very well, going viral. Titled "How Will You Answer?," it featured Melissa Ohden, a survivor of a late-term abortion, and criticized Barack Obama's votes as an Illinois state legislator against protections for infants born alive as a result of failed abortions. But by then, it was too late. The Romney campaign made clear the life issue was not their priority; rank-and-file pro-life voters were demoralized by the Romney-Ryan campaign and had little incentive to go to the polls or work to turn out the pro-life vote. That mighty force was allowed to lie fallow. Romney went into Election Day believing he had momentum. Instead, he got only 47 percent of the vote, losing Florida, Virginia, and Ohio.

CHAPTER 12

They Feel Pain

ACCORDING TO THE TALKING heads who tried to spin Romney's defeat, it happened because he spent too *much* time talking about social issues. In the aftermath of the election, consultant Mike Murphy lamented that the GOP didn't appeal beyond its base. Matthew Dowd, another consultant, said it was time for the GOP to abandon social issues to appeal to Obama's coalition. Even the editors of *National Review* got in on the act: "Too many social conservatives have, however, embraced a self-defeating approach to politics," they fretted.

I wondered if these folks had experienced the same campaign as the rest of us. It seemed as if powerful forces in the GOP needed a scapegoat for Romney's defeat, and if they could purge the party of pesky pro-life agitators in the process, so much the better. The Republican National Committee undertook an "autopsy" on the failed campaign; the elite-driven process concluded, "When it comes to social issues, the Party must in fact and deed be inclusive and welcoming. If we are not, we will limit our ability to attract young people and others, including many women, who agree with us on some but not all issues." In other words, the "truce" was back.

The autopsy's conclusions did not match up with the facts on the ground. In 2012, Gallup found that only 41 percent of Americans identified themselves as pro-choice, a record low. Fifty-one percent called themselves pro-life, one point below its record high. Driving the movement toward pro-life identification are precisely the young people and minorities the GOP hoped to attract. Only 20 percent of voters agreed with the position of Barack Obama and the Democratic Party that abortion should be legal in all circumstances throughout pregnancy. In 2013, Gallup reported that there is no gender gap between men and women on the issue of abortion and that millennials (ages twenty-four to thirty-nine) are the most pro-life generation ever, with 57 percent in favor of making abortion illegal in most or all cases. Only 29 percent of young people adhere to the Democratic Party's abortion agenda. In addition, polls consistently showed a majority of Hispanic voters oppose abortion in most instances.

The American Principles Project issued what came to be known as an "autopsy of the autopsy." Its report, titled *Building a Winning GOP Coalition: Lessons of 2012*, asked, "Facing an incumbent president in the middle of one of the worst economic periods in recent memory, how did the GOP lose in 2012?"

Its answer followed:

We believe the conventional explanation emerging from the Republican National Committee's "autopsy" report gets the core issues exactly wrong. Accepting this emerging conventional wisdom will, in our view, likely consign the GOP to a permanent minority status. The conventional wisdom is this: the national GOP lost in 2012 because extremist social issues hurt GOP candidates by distracting voters from our winning economic message. There are only two problems with this analysis, in our view: First, social issues (especially the life issues) do not hurt GOP candidates . . . they help them win elections. Second, and most importantly, the GOP's economic message as currently structured is not a winning message.

(The APP analysis was largely validated by the 2016 results, when President Trump won on an economic and social platform that a candidate following the GOP autopsy's recommendations would have rejected.)

Rather than retreat in the face of a reemerging push for a social issues truce, SBA List went on offense to set the agenda both electorally and legislatively.

In 2011, SBA List launched a new research and education arm to equip policymakers and the pro-life movement with top-quality science and statistics. For more than forty years, the abortion industry had dominated this arena—no more. Chuck Donovan, whose expertise had shaped public policy through decades of work at the National Right to Life Committee, Family Research Council, and the Heritage Foundation, joined the SBA

List family in 2011 as president of what would become the Charlotte Lozier Institute, named for a trailblazing pro-life, feminist doctor.

Two years later, at Chuck's suggestion, we created the National Pro-life Women's Caucus in order to build pro-life politics among women from the bottom up—the "farm team," so to speak. Marilyn Musgrave traveled nationally to help women who were running for office at the local and state level develop pro-life legislative initiatives to bring before the voters. The 2014 election resulted in the election of 119 women to statewide office, including the governor of Oklahoma, Mary Fallin. This initiative ensures that pro-life women are defending life at the state level and earning the credentials they will need to be successful in national elections.

On the legislative front, we helped transform the Pain-Capable Unborn Child Protection Act from a District of Columbia bill to a national bill. The Pain-Capable Unborn Child Protection Act (H.R. 1797), introduced by Arizona Republican Trent Franks to the 113th Congress on April 26, 2013, had 184 cosponsors, including 13 women. The rationale behind this bill, developed by National Right to Life Committee (NRLC), was the consensus reached among medical researchers that unborn children can feel pain by the fifth month of their development.

SBA List's research and education arm, the Charlotte Lozier Institute, researched global abortion policies. We found that only seven other nations in the world allow abortion after the fifth month of pregnancy, among them some of the world's most brutal regimes—including North Korea, Vietnam, and China—a finding the *Washington Post*'s fact-checkers dubbed "surprisingly true." A broad majority of the American people support this limit—Gallup found nearly two-thirds support drawing the line on abortions after five months. Other polls confirmed broad-based support. A poll by Quinnipiac University showed 60 percent of Americans support a five-month abortion limit; its poll showed 56 percent of Independents and 45 percent of Democrats agreed. A 2013 *Washington Post* poll found that 60 percent of women support this bill. The Pain-Capable bill and the messaging behind it formed the basis of SBA List's offense strategy until Governor Northam came out publicly in support of infanticide in 2019.

The Pain-Capable bill passed the House on June 18, 2013, by a vote of 228 to 196 with only six Republicans voting against it. In a Senate dominated by Democrats, though, it stood little chance of making it to the president's desk, and if it did, it would surely be vetoed.

For SBA List to fully mobilize for the 2014 election, we needed support from donors at a higher level than ever before. Our super PAC, Women Speak Out, set out to assemble and mobilize the largest ever pro-life ground game in key battleground Senate races, including Arkansas, Louisiana, North Carolina, and Kansas. We needed to bring our message directly to the voters and show candidates we could help them win. Every state in which we engaged in required an investment of at least $1,000,000.

Wealthy donors were skeptical at first; we had to convince them that microtargeting pro-lifers could yield results in the same way it had on fiscal matters. SBA List had to persuade donors that we could do it and that mobilizing these voters could help provide the margin of victory.

It worked. During the 2014 campaign, 768 SBA List canvassers made 520,050 visits to voters' homes and made more than a million voter contacts in four states. Our staff members weren't just knocking on random doors—they were targeting identified pro-life voters who don't normally vote in midterm election cycles, bypassing the din of radio and TV ads with face-to-face conversations. What message did we use to educate and motivate these low-propensity voters? We informed them about the liberal candidate's radical support for painful late-term abortions and their support of taxpayer-funded abortion on demand.

A funny thing happened along the way. The more vocal we got about the extreme positions taken by proabortion candidates, the less they talked about the issue. Many Democratic candidates and their support groups shied away from putting the abortion issue front and center. The *Wall Street Journal* reported, "EMILY's List is backing more Senate candidates in the South than ever in its three-decade history. The group, which raises money for Democratic women who support abortion rights, is the largest single contributor to four Southern candidates, including North Carolina's Sen. Kay Hagan. Yet none of them are talking much about abortion, a change from recent elections in which Democrats used the issue to stir female voters." In fact, none of the EMILY's List candidates for any office running in the South ran ads on abortion, including Wendy Davis, a Texas gubernatorial candidate who kick-started her political career by advocating for extreme, unrestricted late-term abortion.

These candidates might not have been talking about their abortion stances—but we were. SBA List won nine of the thirteen contests in which we opposed EMILY's List candidates. None of the four women they supported for the Senate—Kay Hagan (D-NC), Alison Grimes (D-KY), Michelle Nunn (D-GA), and Natalie Tennant (D-WV)—won; the Democrats lost control of the U.S. Senate. Wendy Davis lost as well.

One woman who did win a seat in the Senate was pro-life Joni Ernst of Iowa. A mother, a veteran, and a long-time public servant, Ernst won a hard-fought campaign against proabortion congressman Bruce Braley. Hillary Clinton apparently didn't get the memo about staying mum on abortion; at a campaign event for Braley just before Election Day, she attacked Ernst for her pro-life views: "It is not enough to be a woman. You have to be committed to expand rights and opportunities for all women." Ernst trounced Braley on Election Day 52 to 43 percent and became the first woman elected to either house of Congress from Iowa.

A total of twenty-one pro-life women were elected to the 114th Congress, the largest number in history, a vindication of our strategy. We spent a record $15 million in 2014. Since our founding, SBA List had helped elect more than one hundred pro-life candidates to the U.S. House of Representatives, nineteen to the U.S. Senate, and sixteen to other statewide offices across the country.

Politics thrives on those moments when there is clarity, and there was definitely that in the 2014 results. It was a proof-of-concept moment. At SBA List, we learned that going forward, candidates who employ what they know about their opponents' extremism on abortion and who reframe the issue of life around actual specific legislative proposals will gain an advantage that can lead to victory.

That's a message we have to deliver again and again.

With a record number of pro-life women in the House, SBA List and all our allies looked forward to an early vote on the bill limiting abortion after five months of pregnancy. The vote was scheduled by House leadership to coincide with the forty-first March for Life. But the day before, the bill was suddenly pulled from the floor in a stunning disappointment to the hundreds of thousands of pro-life activists assembled in Washington for the march and millions more around the country.

The controversy centered on an issue that had arisen the year before, when the bill's primary sponsor, Trent Franks, added an exception for rape in instances when the rape was reported to authorities. A handful of GOP women in Congress objected to the way Congressman Franks handled the issue, feeling they had not been consulted or allowed input. We learned of their concerns ten days before the bill was scheduled for a vote in 2014.

Two nights before the Friday vote during the March for Life, SBA List held a reception for new members of Congress at the Capitol Hill Club. Pro-life members of both the House and Senate were in attendance, many of whom we'd helped elect. Those who spoke, including RNC chairman Reince Priebus, celebrated the victory that was at hand, the passage in the House of the 2015 Pain-Capable Unborn Child Protection Act. However, Rep. Trent Franks, the original author of the bill in 2013, appeared nervous, and when I asked him, he expressed concern about the meeting of the House Rules Committee that was underway.

As the SBA List reception wound down, Emily Buchanan told me that House Majority Leader Kevin McCarthy wanted to meet with me in an adjacent room. Together with Chuck Donovan, Marilyn Musgrave, and other pro-life leaders including Concerned Women for America's CEO and president Penny Nance, NRLC's Carol Tobias, the March for Life's Tom McClusky, and Chris Smith and Trent Franks, we crossed the hall to meet with McCarthy. In the hallway, as we walked into the meeting, Congressman Joe Pitts told me the bill was going to be pulled, adding, "They [some of the House women we had helped elect to Congress] think you are bullies!"

Once seated in the room, the first thing McCarthy said was, "You all have some education to do with these women." McCarthy started to describe the situation, but I interrupted, "Are you telling me the bill is dead?"

McCarthy responded by saying he had done everything he could to bring the bill to the floor, including changing the calendar, but he "had to pull the bill" because so many women members had objected to the reporting requirement for rape victims.

Frank Cannon asked McCarthy, "Will you commit to bringing it back on a date certain?" McCarthy said no but that the House was going to vote on another bill, H.R. 7—No Taxpayer Funding for Abortion and Abortion Insurance Full Disclosure Act.

Completely exasperated, I asked, "Do you think that bill is going to make people happy?" The entire pro-life movement had been gearing up for two years for the vote on the Pain-Capable bill, our number-one priority.

McCarthy clearly felt under fire, and he tried to explain that he was unable to convince the women members to reconsider.

I pressed the question: "This is bigger than the House. Do you have any idea what an enormous disaster this is? This bill has been passed in thirteen states, we spent $15 million on this in the last election, and we are finally on the offense . . ."

McCarthy once again appealed for our help: "I know, I changed the calendar—you need to go talk to all these women."

I reminded Rep. McCarthy that this handful of women members could not defeat the bill if he brought it to the floor the next day. We had enough votes to pass it with or without them. All that needed to be done was to introduce a motion to recommit (which provides one final opportunity for the House to debate and amend a measure before the Speaker orders the vote on final passage). He shook his head, saying this would be "too upsetting" to the women members who opposed it. So I asked, "If not tomorrow, then when?" "I can't promise when" was his answer.

Things grew heated rather quickly. Penny Nance reminded Rep. McCarthy, "We are going to cooperate, we are all friends here, but why do you have any impression that it will be any different after these conversations?" All Rep. McCarthy could do was repeat the necessity of going through the process of meeting with the women.

Of course, we did find out that some women members were raising questions. There had been a breakfast meeting at the Capitol ten days before the vote led by Marilyn Musgrave and assisted by Chuck Donovan. Donovan had prepared a two-pager containing polling results and all the talking points needed for the floor debate. The purpose of the meeting was simple, just to touch base with the pro-life women in the House who had expressed their support for the Pain-Capable bill. At this breakfast, we first learned that a number of key pro-life Republican women had objections to the reporting requirements of the bill, but we didn't know they were pressuring leadership to have the bill pulled from a vote on the House floor until the language was changed.

We tried to get in touch with the women right after we heard these concerns but could not reach any of them.

At the time, we thought the reason was the five-day GOP meeting in Hershey, Pennsylvania, starting the day after the breakfast meeting. We heard later that Congresswoman Renee Ellmers of North Carolina had spoken at the retreat, complaining, "The men never listen to us," pointing at pro-life leaders Chris Smith, Joe Pitts, and Steve King.

Ellmers repeated her comment in an interview with *National Journal* that was published on January 16. Ellmers also went on record saying this bill would turn off "millennials," making it clear she did not want it to be the first piece of legislation of the 114th Congress. Ellmers, in fact, was merely repeating the abortion lobby's message about the undesirability of the bill. Ellmers, along with Congresswoman Jackie Walorski of Indiana, withdrew her cosponsorship of the bill.

I couldn't believe at first that Renee Ellmers was the one leading the charge to pull the Pain-Capable bill. When Ellmers first launched her campaign for Congress, SBA List was her first PAC endorsement. As a nurse, she was well aware of the violence of abortion. She did not get in touch with me or anyone in the pro-life movement to address her concerns before launching an all-out effort to kill the bill. She didn't offer an amendment to the bill or take any action to make it better. When another female member tried to reason with Ellmers on the House floor the week before the March for Life, she looked her in the eyes and said, "Go to hell!" In short, Ellmers and her allies played into the worst stereotypes of women in politics—they didn't solve problems, they just threw tantrums.

On the morning of the March for Life, I could barely get out of bed. The previous night had left me feeling traumatized. It felt like déjà vu as I thought back to Stupak's betrayal four years earlier. I sent a text to my friend Penny Nance saying, "I cannot go the March." She shot back, "You are getting back in the fight, now!"

Chastened, I got out of bed, dressed, and went to the March, which was perhaps the most successful in history in terms of the number of people attending—three hundred thousand—along with the size and quality of the media coverage. While there, I ran into a reporter from Breitbart who asked for a comment on the House's action that morning to withdraw the Pain-Capable bill. He asked if there would be a primary challenge to Rep. Renee Ellmers. As I was answering, I realized I was not staying on the talking points of our press release. I responded, "That tidal wave has already begun. That's going to happen, and she deserves it."

In fact, pro-life members of Congress were already feeling blowback from the grassroots for their failure to get the Pain-Capable bill to the floor. Two brand-new members, Elise Stefanik, who represented the New York district in which we had worked to defeat Dede Scozzafava in 2009, and Mia Love of Utah were under the gun from constituents even though they were not part of any effort to derail the bill.

Despite my statement to Breitbart, SBA List decided to release a diplomatic statement, free of the criticism we believed House leadership deserved: "We support Majority Leader McCarthy's call for a prompt vote on the Pain-Capable Unborn Child Protection Act during this Congress, and we will be working with the House Republican leadership to ensure the maximum number of votes." For the time being, we wanted to play an inside strategy. As our strategist Frank Cannon said at the time, we could get off the "inside track" at the point we felt it necessary.

The day after the March for Life, I met with Majority Leader McCarthy and several other pro-life leaders to discuss bringing the bill back to the floor. Once again, McCarthy said nothing could be done until we talked directly to the women members who had changed their minds on the bill—he referred to these meetings as "listening tours." When I asked when the bill was going to be voted on, McCarthy avoided answering.

In the weeks after the sudden pulling of the bill and the subsequent "listening" sessions, a complicated and often frustrating series of meetings were held to discuss revisions to the bill's language. Our primary concern was to not provide a legal loophole that could be used to subvert the intentions of the bill. The SBA List staff worked to help create language that would be accepted by the women members and would in fact strengthen the provisions in the bill. The language about victims of rape and incest was revised, requiring them to receive counseling or medical treatment at least forty-eight hours before having an abortion. Only in the case of minors would abortion providers be required to contact local authorities.

After being told the bill would make it back to the House floor by the time of Pope Francis's visit in September 2015, we were pleasantly surprised when it was reintroduced much sooner. McCarthy was true to his word and came back stronger from this debacle—a committed leader who would repeatedly schedule the bill and name it in honor of Micah Pickering. Finally, on May 13, 2015, the bill was passed in the House by a vote of 242 to 184. Several of the Republican women who were behind the withdrawal of the bill cosponsored and even spoke in favor of this revised one—Marsha Blackburn, Jackie Walorski, Ann Wagner, and even Renee Ellmers. But for Ellmers, the damage with her constituents had already been done; with our help, she lost her Republican primary in 2016 by a thirty-point margin, thereby ending her congressional career.

Some people ask why it was so important to pass the Pain-Capable bill in 2015, given that it would never become law during an Obama presidency. It was important because Congress was directly challenging the *Roe v. Wade* decision, saying that, at a minimum, unborn babies deserve the protection of the law after five months of fetal life.

The five-month limit also marked a drastic change in the political debate by making clear to voters the current state of the law and the kind of laws that could be enacted if a pro-life president were in the White House. GOP candidates began turning the tables when discussing abortion, asking, Who are the real extremists: the majority of Americans, who support a five-month limit, or those who support abortion until moments before actual birth? The passage of the Pain-Capable Unborn Child Protection Act succeeded in providing a prism through which the radically proabortion core of the Democratic Party could be clearly seen. Against the demonstrable pain felt by an unborn baby aborted at five months or later, the Left's usual rhetoric about "choice" and "women's bodies" sounded hollow, out of date, and unspeakably cruel.

CHAPTER 13

The Abortion Industry Exposed

THE CRUEL REALITY OF abortion stands in stark contrast to the euphemisms its supporters use to describe it. None is more absurd than the claim that abortion is an issue of "women's health." Leaving aside the critical fact that 50 percent of the victims of abortion are girls, the abortion procedure itself often harms the physical and psychological health of the women who endure it and sometimes results in their death.

The case of Dr. Kermit Gosnell, later made into a feature film, vividly illustrates the harm done to women's health and lives by abortion. Gosnell ran an abortion facility in West Philadelphia called the Women's Medical Society, an Orwellian misuse of language if ever there was one. In fact, as was detailed in a trial that resulted in his conviction for the murder of three newborn children and the involuntary manslaughter of a mother, Gosnell's operation was truly a "house of horrors." According to a 281-page grand jury report that led to Gosnell's indictment, "The premises were dirty and unsanitary. Gosnell routinely relied on unlicensed and untrained staff to treat patients, conduct medical tests, and administer medications without supervision. Even more alarmingly, Gosnell instructed unlicensed workers to sedate patients with dangerous drugs in his absence...."

In addition, he regularly performed abortions beyond the 24-week limit prescribed by [a Pennsylvania] law. As a result, viable babies were born. Gosnell killed them by plunging scissors into their spinal cords. He taught his staff to do the same."

The trial exposed the gross negligence of the Pennsylvania Department of Health, which despite receiving numerous complaints about Gosnell's practices failed to inspect his facility for more than seventeen years. The grand jury report explains, "After 1993 . . . the Pennsylvania Department of Health abruptly decided, for political reasons, to stop inspecting abortion clinics at all. The politics in question were not anti-abortion, but pro. With the change of administration from Governor Casey to Governor Ridge, officials concluded that inspections would be 'putting a barrier up to women' seeking abortions." Simply put, when governor Tom Ridge, a "pro-choice" Republican, replaced governor Bob Casey, a Democrat and a longtime pro-life champion, Kermit Gosnell was given free rein.

Tragically, Gosnell is not an outlier. There are numerous documented cases of negligence, maternal death, and infanticide in abortion facilities around the country run by so-called doctors like James Pendergraft, Ulrich Klopfer, and Steven Brigham. The complicity of the media in covering up that reality was put on full display in the Gosnell case. Columnist Kirsten Powers wrote in *USA Today*,

> Infant beheadings. Severed baby feet in jars. A child screaming after it was delivered alive during

an abortion procedure. Haven't heard about these sickening accusations? It's not your fault. Since the murder trial of Pennsylvania abortion doctor Kermit Gosnell began March 18, there has been precious little coverage of the case that should be on every news show and front page. The revolting revelations of Gosnell's former staff, who have been testifying to what they witnessed and did during late-term abortions, should shock anyone with a heart. . . . The deafening silence of too much of the media, once a force for justice in America, is a disgrace.

When the *Federalist*'s Mollie Hemingway asked the *Washington Post*'s health reporter Sarah Kliff why the *Post* had ignored the Gosnell trial, she replied it was because she did not cover local crime stories. Looking back on the exchange three years later, Hemingway wrote, "Gosnell's horrific abortion clinic conditions and the legislation they spawned became the biggest abortion policy story of the next few years. But the one consistent thing about the media approach was the extreme downplaying of Gosnell and other abortion clinics with unsafe and unsanitary conditions."

In the aftermath of the Gosnell case, several states took action to ensure that abortion facilities operating in their states met minimum standards of health and safety. One such law in Texas required abortion facili-ties to meet the standards for ambulatory surgery centers and to require physicians to have admitting privileges to a hospital within a thirty-mile radius of their operations. These justifiable safeguards were designed to protect the life and health of women who undergo abortions. In fact, treating abortion sites as ambulatory surgical centers was specifically recommended by the grand jury that reviewed the tragic errors Pennsylvania made.

I still can't comprehend how abortion advocates get away with opposing this and similar laws. One of their main arguments in favor of legal abortion is that it prevents dangerous "back-alley" abortions. How is legal abortion impeded by ensuring the facilities that provide it are sanitary, safe, and staffed by competent medical professionals? In upholding the Texas law, the Fifth Circuit Court of Appeals found that these requirements placed no "undue burden" on women or their "right" to an abortion.

Yet oppose the Texas law is precisely what abortion advocates did, appealing the circuit court ruling to the United States Supreme Court. By agreeing to review *Whole Women's Health v. Hellerstedt* in 2015, the court for the first time in nearly a decade would hear arguments challenging the constitutionality of state laws regulating abortion. SBA List filed an amicus brief with the court in support of the Texas law. But in June 2016, the court ruled five to three that the Texas law was unconstitutional. Once again, the muddled mind of Justice Anthony Kennedy provided the margin of victory for the abortion lobby; given the absence of a ninth justice since Antonin Scalia's death in February, a four-to-four tie would have allowed the circuit court's ruling to stand.

In a statement on the day of the ruling, I wrote, "The abortion industry cannot be trusted to regulate itself and they know it. That's why they fought tooth and nail against common-sense health and safety standards and requirements for abortionists to have admitting privileges at nearby hospitals. We have documented page after page of incidents of abuse, negligence, and brutality since 2008. This decision means the filth and exploitation will continue unchecked."

Justice Ruth Bader Ginsburg's opinion striking down the Texas law read in part, "When a State severely limits access to safe and legal procedures, women in desperate circumstances may resort to unlicensed rogue practitioners . . . at great risk to their health and safety." In other words, requiring abortion facilities to be medically safe and sanitary forces women to go to facilities that are not safe and sanitary. The incoherence would be laughable if the consequence were not so tragic.

Mollie Hemingway again summed it up:

> But just on the issue of regulatory oversight of clinics, the media are perpetuating a closed loop. The abortion corporations' claim is that abortion clinics are safe and wonderful, but that they will somehow be forced to close if required to hold the same health and safety standards as other surgery centers. They carry water for the abortion corporations, fighting any oversight of abortion-related practices. They smother-to-the-death any and all stories about unsafe

and unsanitary conditions at health clinics. They mock voters who don't get their marching orders from Planned Parenthood and other abortion corporations. They praise Supreme Court justices who run roughshod over the law to keep at bay any regulation of abortion clinics. Rinse, repeat.

Rinse, repeat, indeed. The same dynamic applied to the revelations beginning in the summer of 2015 that Planned Parenthood, by far the nation's largest abortion business, engaged systematically in the sale of fetal body parts obtained from the babies they killed.

In a heartbreaking series of undercover videos, the Center for Medical Progress (CMP) exposed the ugly truth of Planned Parenthood's business model. By its own admission, Planned Parenthood performs more than 345,000 abortions a year—many at a point when babies can survive outside the womb. They also "harvest" brains, livers, hearts, and other organs from the remains of the babies they have aborted and, for a fee, provide them to for-profit companies that remarket them, even more profitably, for medical research.

Among the many chilling moments captured on video is Planned Parenthood Federation of America's director of medical services, Dr. Deborah Nucatola, crunching her salad and sipping a glass of red wine while she describes the best techniques for dismembering unborn babies in order to obtain top dollar for their intact body parts: "We've been very good at getting heart, lung, liver, because we know that, so I'm not gonna crush that part, I'm gonna basically crush below, I'm gonna crush above, and I'm gonna see if I can get it all intact."

Another video shows Planned Parenthood executive Dr. Mary Gatter negotiating the price of baby body parts with the people posing undercover as executives of a bio-tech firm, joking that she needs the best price because she wants to buy a Lamborghini.

The House of Representatives moved quickly to pass legislation stripping Planned Parenthood of the half-billion dollars in taxpayer funds it receives each year, redirecting those funds instead to community health centers that do not provide abortions, and to convene a select committee to investigate the abuses. Congress-woman Marsha Blackburn of Tennessee, a strong ally of SBA List whom we helped elect in 2002, was chosen to lead the committee. The Senate followed suit, defunding Planned Parenthood in a budget reconciliation bill that also repealed key parts of Obamacare.

But the horror uncovered by CMP did not fully break into the national conversation until Carly Fiorina, dur-ing a 2015 Republican primary debate, her voice full of passion, said, "I dare Hillary Clinton and Barack Obama to watch these tapes. Watch a fully formed fetus on the table. Its heart beating. Its legs kicking while someone says we have to keep it alive to harvest its brain. This is about the character of our nation."

After a year-long investigation, the House select com-mittee released a report documenting exactly how the abortion industry sells baby hearts, livers, brains, hands, and other body parts. A middleman sets up shop in their facilities, paying for the "privilege" of obtaining body parts that it then resells for tens of thousands of dollars more, depending on the child's characteristics. Was the developing baby eighteen weeks old? Twenty-four weeks? Was the mother a smoker? What is the child's ethnicity? All these factors might make the heart, foot, eyeball, or limbs more expensive. Procurement technicians are trained to work with clinic staff to target women coming in for abortions based on gestational age. They are told to quickly obtain consent from women at one of the most vulnerable points in their lives, relying on consent forms that are at best misleading about the likelihood of "cures" resulting from research using fresh baby organs. The procurement technicians are promised bonuses for particular baby parts, with stomachs, bladders, and lungs resulting in a higher per-item bonus than ears, kidneys, or tongues.

The CMP videos powerfully confirmed the truth about Planned Parenthood, one it works assiduously to conceal: its business is abortion, not women's health care. Indeed, a look at the organization's history reveals that its primary objective has never been serving the health needs of disadvantaged women and families but something much darker.

Planned Parenthood founder Margaret Sanger wrote in the *New York Times* in 1923 that her goal was the "release and cultivation of the better elements in our society and the gradual suppression, elimination and eventual extinction of defective stock—those human weeds which threaten the blossoming of the finest flowers of American civilization." Today that eugenic mission is carried out through discriminatory abortions targeting babies diagnosed with genetic diseases, a practice that is putting children born with Down syndrome on the road to extinction, as is already happening in Iceland. The abortion industry's most frequent victims in the United States are African Americans; 38 percent of all abortions are performed on black women, even though they make up only about 14 percent of the female population in America—a disparity that has increased even as the overall abortion rate has decreased significantly thanks to pro-life efforts. In New York City, which has one of the nation's highest abortion rates, more black babies are aborted than born alive—an unfathomable tragedy for this community that has suffered and overcome so many injustices.

In terms of the provision of legitimate health care services, the abortion giant is an insignificant player. Charlotte Lozier Institute found that Planned Parenthood provides just 1 percent of HIV tests and Pap tests performed in America but dominates the abortion market, carrying out approximately 40 percent of all abortions in the nation. The pro-life group Live Action called Planned Parenthood facilities and found ninety-two of ninety-seven admitted they don't do any prenatal care at all. "No, we don't do prenatal services. I mean, it's called Planned Parenthood, I know it's kind of deceiving," a Merrillville, Indiana, Planned Parenthood worker confessed. Its former president, Cecile Richards, even had to admit under oath that her organization does not do mammograms, as is so often claimed in its defense. In 2019, Richards's successor was fired after less than a year for attempting to steer the organization away from abortion as its central mission—if not in practice, at least in word.

I met David Daleiden, the man behind the videos that sparked a national conversation on late-term abortion and the true priorities of the abortion industry, at a conference in California in July 2015, soon after the first video was released. The videos were a complete surprise to me and to many others in the pro-life movement; behind the scenes, this courageous, creative, and brilliant man had built a devastating case against the abortion industry, using the words of its own high priestesses to expose the moral rot at its core. He had the quiet calm of a solitary monk who recently emerged from the desert. I was amazed by the story of this man taking years out of his young life to prepare for and live out his deep cover as a part of the abortion industry in order to bring its crimes to light, and I was humbled by his trust and optimism that justice would be done.

The abortion industry, unable to refute or defend what was revealed in the CMP videos, struck back at the messenger with fury, challenging Daleiden's serenity and confidence. Adversaries filed politically motivated criminal charges against Daleiden in Texas and California. Although the Texas charges were dropped, Daleiden and his colleague Sandra Merritt were hit with fifteen felony charges in California state court in a criminal case initiated by then attorney general Kamala Harris and taken up by her successor, Xavier Becerra—both abortion industry allies. Six of those charges were subsequently dropped. Apparently in California, the First Amendment rights of journalists to work undercover don't extend to pro-lifers; even the *Los Angeles Times* editorialized that it is "disturbingly aggressive for Becerra to apply this criminal statute to people who were trying to influence a contested issue of public policy." Even so, the trial elicited a stunning testimony that a Planned Parenthood baby parts buyer sold the "beating hearts" and fully intact heads of innocent children killed in potentially illegal abortions. Meanwhile, Planned Parenthood and the National Abortion Federation filed civil lawsuits in federal court. In a profoundly unjust verdict engineered by a proabortion activist judge, CMP was ordered to pay Planned Parenthood more than $2.2 million in damages. CMP's fight continues.

In 2016, pro-life voters helped elect a pro-life president, who explicitly promised to defund Planned Parenthood. What could be more emblematic of the "swamp" in need of draining than an organization that donates millions to politicians to influence their votes in favor of a half-billion-dollar yearly subsidy from the taxpayer? The subsidy is spent to maintain the nation's largest abortion network, which uses abortions to increase revenue—a horrifying practice exposed by former Planned Parenthood director and pro-life convert Abby Johnson in 2011—and supplements that income by illegally selling off the body parts of the unborn babies it kills, as revealed in the CMP videos.

While many important pro-life legislative initiatives face the hurdle of requiring a supermajority to avoid a filibuster in the Senate, it only takes a simple majority to stop taxpayer subsidies to Planned Parenthood through a budget reconciliation bill that cannot be filibustered. With pro-life majorities in the House and Senate who had voted to defund Planned Parenthood in the past and a president who campaigned on a promise to sign the bill, it should have been an easy and quick victory.

Instead, Planned Parenthood funding wound up being part of a larger effort to repeal Obamacare, including its expansion of abortion funding, the issue that so many pro-life Democrats had lost their seats over in 2010. As I sat with David Daleiden and Frank Cannon outside the Senate chamber late at night in July 2017, lobbying senators as they shuttled in and out, the outcome of the vote was more in doubt than it should have been. Senator John McCain dramatically cast the deciding vote with a thumbs-down gesture. Obamacare's abortion funding and Planned Parenthood's taxpayer subsidy would—for the time being, at least—remain in place. But McCain's vote would have been meaningless if it were not for the votes of two proabortion *women* senators—Republicans Susan Collins of Maine and Lisa Murkowski of Alaska. SBA List, since its founding, helped elect dozens of pro-life women to the House, Senate, and statewide office and defeated as many proabortion women. But the fact that there still are women in Congress who buy into the lie that feminism requires women to sacrifice their own children at the altar of abortion means we still have work to do.

CHAPTER 14

Fighting to Win

IF THE 2016 ELECTION was a watershed moment for the pro-life movement, 2020 is the most consequential election in nearly half a century since *Roe v. Wade*.

I'm often asked, "What do pro-lifers want for their votes?" They want leaders who will fearlessly and without apology fight for the lives of unborn babies and their mothers—who will place the right to life above or on par with other great national issues of economic strength and national security. The great pro-life Congressman Henry Hyde once told an incoming class of freshmen House members that defending the unborn is an issue worth losing an election for. He was right. More importantly, life has become the definitive issue—one that is eminently *winnable*.

Democratic Party leaders took it for granted that the Republican nominee in 2016 would hide his pro-life light under a bushel, as Romney, McCain, Bush, and so many others had done. They were used to the party's candidates engaging in an unconditional surrender on abortion. They did not expect to have their extremism laid bare to a national audience, as Trump did in the third presidential debate against Hillary Clinton. Trump forced Clinton to defend abortion on demand up to the point of birth.

Voters who heard the exchange concluded, as Trump said, "That's not OK with me."

Four years later, President Trump has beyond delivered on his promises to the voters who propelled him to victory, governing as the most pro-life president in history, backed by Vice President Pence and a pro-life Cabinet that includes Alex Azar, Mike Pompeo, William Barr, and others. Impressively, he has done so even in the face of a divided Congress and the efforts of proabortion Democrats to nullify the will of the voters by impeaching and removing him from office—another page from the playbook they had used to try to block Justice Kavanaugh.

The 2018 midterm elections were a clear victory for the pro-life movement. Starting in July of 2017, well before the election was on most Americans' minds, SBA List set out to expand the pro-life majority in the U.S. Senate. We aimed to defeat vulnerable Democrat senators in states President Trump had carried in 2016, focusing on senators who had poor records on key pro-life votes: Bill Nelson in Florida, Joe Donnelly in Indiana, Claire McCaskill in Missouri, Jon Tester in Montana, Heidi Heitkamp in North Dakota, and Joe Manchin in West Virginia. We also had boots on the ground in Arizona and Tennessee to support Martha McSally and former representative Marsha Blackburn in their races for open Senate seats. Our field team of more than 1,100 canvassers visited the homes of 2.7 million inconsistent pro-life voters across nine states, more than doubling our outreach in the previous election cycle.

The result: hundreds of thousands of voters who don't typically vote in midterm elections delivered for pro-life candidates. Four weak incumbent senators were unseated. In Florida, Rick Scott prevailed over Bill Nelson by a margin of slightly more than ten thousand votes; in West Virginia, Joe Manchin likely held onto his seat only because of his last-minute decision to vote to confirm Justice Kavanaugh. Newly elected pro-life Senators Kevin Cramer, Marsha Blackburn, Josh Hawley, Rick Scott, and Mike Braun, among others, distinguished themselves from their radical opponents by going on offense for life throughout their campaigns. Not only is there a pro-life majority in the Senate—a resounding affirmation of President Trump's pro-life agenda—but that majority now includes five strong pro-life women, compared to zero in 2010. It is refreshing to see this progress, a fruit of years of work by SBA List's army of devoted staff, canvassers, and grassroots members across the nation.

That wasn't all. With our help, pro-life champions defeated abortion extremists to gain or maintain control of governorships in Iowa, Florida, Ohio, and Georgia. Iowa governor Kim Reynolds, one of the first governors in America to sign legislation protecting unborn babies as soon as their heartbeat can be detected, defeated former Planned Parenthood board member Fred Hubbell. In Alabama and West Virginia—two out of three states where abortion was directly on the ballot—pro-life state constitutional amendments passed by wide margins. SBA List held four press conferences across the Mountain State as a part of a $500,000 education campaign to pass Amendment 1, which saves the lives of fifteen hundred unborn children in the state every year by stopping Medicaid funding of abortion on demand. Pro-life momentum in the states was clearly on the upswing.

Unfortunately, victory in the Senate and the states was tempered by the loss of the House. With Nancy Pelosi and proabortion Democrats in charge, pro-lifers would need to be constantly on guard against attempts to roll back President Trump's pro-life gains as well as assaults on long-standing policies like the Hyde Amendment. On day one of the new Congress, the Democrats proved radical abortion expansion would be their priority, using legislation meant to fund the federal government to try to repeal the expanded Mexico City policy. This would have forced American taxpayers to subsidize the exportation of abortion around the world via groups that aggressively lobby against the pro-life values and cultural norms of other nations and even facilitate illegal abortions. House Democrats would spend the entirety of 2019 blocking extremely popular legislation to protect babies who survive abortions, introduced by Rep. Ann Wagner (R-MO) in response to Governor Northam and radical efforts in the commonwealth as well as in New York to strip away all such protections. In a seldom-used procedural move, House Republican whip Steve Scalise of Louisiana filed a discharge petition that would force a vote on the House floor if a majority of members signed on. Thanks to the extraordinary obstruction of the Pelosi Democrats, his petition has languished just a handful of signatures away from the necessary 218. Republican members of

Congress, going to the floor at least eighty times to request a vote, have had their microphones abruptly shut off. House Democratic leadership even denied their colleagues available rooms to hold a hearing. Undeterred, the Republicans held their hearing in the Capitol Visitor Center. Frustrated by similar gridlock and perceiving the need, Senator Steve Daines (R-MT) was inspired to launch the first-ever Senate Pro-Life Caucus. To veteran pro-life activists whose memory encompasses so many past betrayals at the hands of lukewarm Republicans, the transformation of the GOP into a party that prioritizes and energetically defends the right to life is among the most dramatic political success stories in the history of this movement—a vindication of SBA List's "offense" strategy.

President Trump continues to be the number-one supporter of legislation to stop late-term abortion and infanticide, urging Congress to act and calling out extremists at every opportunity. In January 2020, he became the first president ever to address the annual March for Life—the nation's largest pro-life event—in person. *Washington Post* columnist Marc Thiessen explained well the significance of the president's embrace of the movement:

> Trump will be greeted as a pro-life hero, because he is one. He put two outstanding conservative justices on the Supreme Court and has appointed a record number of federal appeals court judges. He has allowed states to defund Planned Parenthood, defunded the pro-abortion U.N. Population Fund, and restored and expanded a ban, known as the Mexico City

policy, on taxpayer funds for groups that perform abortions overseas. He has exempted organizations, such as the Little Sisters of the Poor, that have moral objections to providing abortifacient drugs, from the Obamacare Health and Human Services mandate, and he has stood by the nuns as they fight to protect their religious liberty in the Supreme Court.

The president recently delivered the biggest blow to Planned Parenthood in three decades when he implemented the Protect Life Rule, which prohibits Title X family-planning funds from going to any clinic that performs on-site abortions. Planned Parenthood announced last year that it would leave the Title X program, barring a court victory.

No other president has amassed such a record of pro-life victories. But Trump has done more than simply govern as a pro-life conservative; he has embraced pro-life conservatives without shame or hesitation.

On the morning of the march, the Trump campaign announced the launch of Pro-life Voices for Trump. The campaign had invited me to lead the president's pro-life coalition again as national cochair, together with Father Frank Pavone of Priests for Life—a role I was honored to reprise. President Trump now has a proven record to run on, and the wins keep coming. I was also speaking at the rally before the march and had the honor of joining the president on stage, along with Alveda King; Melissa Ohden; Catherine Glenn Foster, president of

Americans United for Life; Louisiana state representative Katrina Jackson, a fearless African American pro-life Democrat and member of our National Pro-life Women's Caucus; and other national and state pro-life leaders. Peering over the president's shoulder as he delivered one of the most stirring pro-life speeches of his presidency to date, it was evident to me that he was truly speaking from the heart:

> All of us here today understand an eternal truth: Every child is a precious and sacred gift from God. Together, we must protect, cherish, and defend the dignity and sanctity of every human life.
>
> When we see the image of a baby in the womb, we glimpse the majesty of God's creation. When we hold a newborn in our arms, we know the endless love that each child brings to a family. When we watch a child grow, we see the splendor that radiates from each human soul. One life changes the world.

President Trump highlighted the youthfulness of the pro-life movement; young people have for years composed a large and growing contingent of marchers. He praised the heroism of moms who choose life, often in the most difficult circumstances, and the selfless volunteers at the front lines of America's network of pro-life pregnancy centers—more than 2,600 of which, staffed mostly by volunteers, provide nearly two million people a year with vital services free of charge. The president spoke of the love that animates and sustains our movement, our reason for being that has allowed us to persevere for nearly half a century:

> We cannot know what our citizens yet unborn will achieve, the dreams they will imagine, the masterpieces they will create, the discoveries they will make. But we know this: Every life brings love into this world. Every child brings joy to a family. Every person is worth protecting. And above all, we know that every human soul is divine, and every human life—born and unborn—is made in the holy image of Almighty God.
>
> Together, we will defend this truth all across our magnificent land. We will set free the dreams of our people. And with determined hope, we look forward to all of the blessings that will come from the beauty, talent, purpose, nobility, and grace of every American child.

It is never easy to speak after the president of the United States, but his presence and thoughtful words left us inspired. I wanted to invite the pilgrims there to take stock of our moment in history, the moral and legal precipice at which America stands forty-seven long years after *Roe*, and to impress on them a sense of hope and possibility—and urgency. The 2020 elections coincide with the centennial celebration of the Nineteenth Amendment securing women's right to vote and the brave women and men who fought for that right. In equating abortion with liberation, the power of the women's movement has been misused to enormously harmful effect. Now is the time to use the power of the ballot box to turn back that harm and begin the process of healing the wounds of our nation.

The mainstream media have a long history of neglecting the March for Life in their coverage, but they could not ignore the president. In an interview with reporters from the *New York Times*, I explained how President Trump wasn't only taking the fight to his proabortion Democratic opponents; he represents an emerging new class of Republican—fully engaged and energized on the life issue like never before: "The difference between 2016 and now is how fully the Republican Party has accepted the [pro-life] issue as a driving force at the center of elections. . . . This president is the reason why. He took it on, put it at the center of his campaign-fulfilled promises and is putting this cause at the center of his re-election this year." The story's headline read, "Trump Tells Anti-abortion Marchers, 'Unborn Children Have Never Had a Stronger Defender in the White House.'" I couldn't agree more.

President Trump's leadership stands in stark contrast to today's Democrats. The Democratic presidential primary quickly became a contest to see which candidate could prove to be the most radically proabortion. In the summer of 2019, twenty Democratic contenders lined up to compete for support from the abortion lobby at a forum in South Carolina hosted by Planned Parenthood. Julián Castro, former HUD secretary under

President Obama, was widely mocked for a statement in the first Democratic primary debate that seemed to endorse taxpayer-funded abortions for biological men: "Just because a woman, or let's also not forget someone in the trans community—a trans female—is poor, doesn't mean they shouldn't exercise that right to choose." New York senator Kirsten Gillibrand went even further in an interview with the *Des Moines Register*, likening millions of Americans' deeply held pro-life convictions to racism: "I think there's some issues that have such moral clarity that we have as a society decided that the other side is not acceptable. . . . Imagine saying that it's OK to appoint a judge who's racist, or anti-Semitic, or homophobic. . . . I don't think those are political issues anymore."

More than anyone, Joe Biden exemplified his party's race to the left. When he reversed his position on the Hyde Amendment after decades of opposition to taxpayer funding of abortion, the Democratic Party's capitulation to the radical abortion lobby was complete. The days of "safe, legal, and rare" were history, and now it was a foregone conclusion that no matter who won the caucuses or the primaries, the eventual Democratic Party nominee would be an extremist who supports taxpayer-funded abortion on demand through the moment of birth and even infanticide.

Most Americans—including many rank-and-file Democrats—disagree with this agenda. In 2017, Gallup found 71 percent of Americans do not share the abortion movement's support for abortion on demand in all circumstances. Sixty-four percent of *women* want abortion to be illegal in some or all circumstances. As of 2019, Gallup found 51 percent of women identify themselves as pro-life. Polling released by SBA List showed that 64 percent of voters support laws to prohibit abortion after five months, when a baby can demonstrably feel pain. Support is especially high among women voters (67 percent), Hispanics (57 percent), African Americans (70 percent), and millennials (78 percent). Shortly after Biden's flip-flop, SBA List released the results of a new poll finding that a majority (50 percent) of voters were less likely to support Biden, including 55 percent of Independent voters, who might be inclined to back a supposed moderate.

The Democrats have a divided house, struggling to recover the soul of their party. Even after decades of relentless effort by the Democratic Party to show pro-lifers the door, polls have shown that as many as one-third of Democrats consider themselves pro-life and more than half of registered Democrats support a five-month Pain-Capable ban. As late as 2017, some party leaders bristled at the idea of imposing harsh litmus tests, such as Democratic National Committee chairman Tom Perez's statement that party orthodoxy in favor of abortion on demand is "nonnegotiable." Pelosi, who in 2013 called late-term abortions "sacred ground," responded that her party should impose no litmus tests on abortion; she'd prefer it to go away, saying, "The issue's fading, it really is." Abortion advocates were incensed. NARAL president Ilyse Hogue, who spoke proudly of her own abortion of convenience at the party's 2016 convention, blasted Pelosi, tweeting, "No, Leader Pelosi, we cannot and will not win elections by sacrificing women's fundamental rights." Democrats running for president in 2020 fell in line. Asked at a town hall in January 2020 whether there is room for pro-lifers in the Democratic Party, former South Bend "Mayor Pete" Buttigieg could not identify a single circumstance in which he would limit abortion or even hear debate on the issue within his party. He was joined shortly by Bernie Sanders, who declared support for abortion "an absolutely essential part of being a Democrat." This may be the election that finally pushes remaining pro-life Democrats to the breaking point.

I hope the Democratic Party returns to its pro-life roots and embraces the vision, laid out so eloquently by the late governor Bob Casey, of a nation that cares for mothers and children. It is long overdue for both major parties to adopt a principled stance in favor of life. Make no mistake, though: the person most responsible for the Democrats' (and our nation's) soul searching on the issue of life is Donald Trump. Nancy Pelosi told the *Washington Post* the life issue was essential to Trump's victory: "That's why Donald Trump is president of the United States—the evangelicals and the Catholics, anti-marriage equality, anti-choice. That's how he got to be president. Everything was trumped, literally and figuratively by that."

The stakes of the 2020 elections are even higher than in 2016. The possibility of another Supreme Court vacancy—one that could tip the scales even further in favor of eroding *Roe*—looms large. It is arguably the biggest motivating factor in congressional Democrats' drive to delegitimize President Trump's election, undo his prolife policy victories, and stop him from winning a second term. President Trump understands; as he has told me more than once and as he perceptively told the crowd gathered on the National Mall for the March, "They are coming after me because I am fighting for you, and we are fighting for those who have no voice." The abortion lobby understands *Roe*'s days are numbered. So must we.

More than any other president before him, President Trump has put the end of abortion in reach. As my friend Vice President Pence is fond of saying, life is winning in America. When we win elections, we change laws that in turn will help restore to America a culture that respects life, supports mothers, and nurtures babies at every stage of development—a nation in which the founders' vision of an "inalienable right to life" for every person, from conception to natural death, is a reality.

No president or political leader, however bold, can fulfill such an aspirational vision alone. Speaking at SBA List's gala in May 2017, Vice President Pence said,

> I truly believe we've come to a pivotal moment in the life of this movement—in the life of our nation. And in this moment, President Trump needs all of you to let your voices be heard—to continue to stand up and speak out, as if it's the most important moment in the history of our movement, because it is. We need

every ounce of your energy and enthusiasm. We need your determination and conviction, your passion, and we need your prayers. We need you to continue to embody the spirit of Susan B. Anthony—the namesake of this organization and our gala tonight, the great defender of women's rights.

This *is* the pivotal moment, and no one who cares can fail to engage. Like every successful human rights movement before us in our nation's history, we must leverage the tools of our democracy. SBA List will redouble our ground efforts to reelect President Trump and protect the crucial pro-life Senate majority, reaching out not only to our base but also to Independents and Democrats who are repelled by the party line. Already, our canvassers are well on their way to making at least four million visits to voters in key battleground states—the most ambitious pro-life ground game yet. The pro-life movement will push to at last defund Planned Parenthood and prevent taxpayer funds from subsidizing the abortion industry through federal health care programs. We will work for judges at all levels who uphold the constitutional right to life. We will fight to pass laws protecting women from dangerous abortion facilities and to protect babies from painful late-term abortions. We will continue working to defeat abortion extremism and elect pro-life champions, women and men, to public office. We will prepare in earnest to receive mothers in crisis with care and compassion and to welcome precious children whose lives have been spared—each little boy or girl irreplaceable and intended for this world, with a purpose only he or she can fulfill. And we will not rest until *Roe v. Wade* is reversed and abortion is no longer the law of our great and good land.

Acknowledgments

WITH GRATITUDE TO GRANNAH and my parents Billy and Hansy Jones who gave me life and a great love for pursuing the truths of it. They, along with my brothers Alan and Larry, also gave the gift that gets better with giving: unconditional love.

My family: Marty, Hannah, Joseph, Elizabeth, Tommy and Terry, for inspiring, challenging and supporting at every step.

Susan Gibbs and Rachel McNair for invitation into the sisterhood.

Jane Abraham and Susan Hirschmann, for beginning and enduring guidance along with the rest of Susan B. Anthony List's Board's wise and generous governance.

My partners Emily Buchanan and Frank Cannon for gift of themselves and immense talents applied to strategy and tactics, finding and forcing inflection points towards victory for life.

Chuck Donovan, Marilyn Musgrave, Billy Valentine, Mallory Quigley, Jennifer Gross, and the Susan B. Anthony List, Charlotte Lozier Institute, Women Speak Out, and Life Issues Institute teams who with great ambition, expertise and sacrifice are making good on the promises of our founding documents.

Mary Cannon, our senior writer Nicole Stacy, and Deal Hudson for your literary prowess.

Further Reading

Chapter 1

Interview in *Christianity Today*, June 1979, pp. 14–19.

Andrew Harmon, "The World According to Nancy Pelosi." *Advocate*, January 12, 2012. https://www.advocate.com/print -issue/cover-stories/2012/01/12/world-accordingnancy-pelosi.

Full text of President Trump's 2019 State of the Union address: https://www.whitehouse.gov/briefings-statements/president -donald-j-trumps-state-union-address-2/.

YouTube video of Tran's testimony: https://www.youtube.com/ watch?v=OMFzZ5I30dg.

Interview on WTOP's *Ask the Governor* segment, January 30, 2019. https://wtop.com/local-politics-elections-news/2019/ 01/va-gov-northam-draws-outrage-from-gop-for-defending -abortion-bill/.

Gallup, multiple years: https://news.gallup.com/poll/1576/ abortion.aspx.

CNN exit poll, November 2016. https://www.cnn.com/election/
    2016/results/exit-polls.
Speech at the Catholic Information Center on October 26, 2016.
    Published by *National Review*, October 27, 2016. https://www
    .nationalreview.com/2016/10/antonin-scalia-faith-law/.
Mary Krane Derr, Rachel MacNair, and Linda Naranjo-Huebl,
    Pro-life Feminism: Yesterday and Today.
"Fact Sheet: Science of Fetal Pain." Charlotte Lozier Institute.
    https://lozierinstitute.org/fact-sheet-science-of-fetal-pain/.
Pam Belluck, "Premature Babies May Survive at 22 Weeks If
    Treated, Study Finds." *New York Times*, May 6, 2015. https://
    www.nytimes.com/2015/05/07/health/premature-babies-22
    -weeks-viability-study.html.
https://melissaohden.com/about/.
https://www.christinabennett.com/#about-me-section.
Drew Daudelin, "Indiana Senate to Consider Bill Restricting
    Abortions." WBAA, January 27, 2020. https://www.wbaa
    .org/post/indiana-senate-consider-bill-restricting-abortions
    #stream/0.

Chapter 2

"2015–2016 Annual Report." Planned Parenthood. https://
    www.plannedparenthood.org/uploads/filer_public/18/
    40/1840b04b-55d3-4c00-959d-11817023ffc8/20170526
    _annualreport_p02_singles.pdf.
Jeremy Peters, "Conservatives Hone Script to Light a Fire over
    Abortion." *New York Times*, July 24, 2014. https://www
    .nytimes.com/2014/07/25/us/politics/republicans-abortion
    -midterm-elections.html?_r=0.
Laura Bassett, "Jeb Bush Is to the Right of George W. on
    Abortion." Huffington Post, March 25, 2015. https://www
    .huffpost.com/entry/jeb-bush-abortion_n_6940568.
Andrew Buncombe, "Jeb Bush: The Republican Candidate's
    Views on Immigration, Abortion and Planned Parenthood."

Independent, August 6, 2015. https://www.independent.co
.uk/news/world/americas/jeb-bush-republican-candidate
-immigration-abortion-planned-parenthood-medicare
-womens-health-10443482.html.

Speech given February 1, 2012: https://www.sba-list.org/rubio.

https://www.congress.gov/bill/106th-congress/house-bill/2436.

https://www.congress.gov/bill/108th-congress/house-bill/1997.

Speech given April 16, 2015: https://www.sba-list.org/suzy-b
-blog/lindsey-grahams-speech-2016-sba-gala.

Valerie Richardson, "Wisconsin Gov. Walker Signs Bills to
Defund Planned Parenthood Affiliate." *Washington Times*,
February 18, 2016. https://www.washingtontimes.com/news/
2016/feb/18/wis-gov-signs-defund-planned-parenthood
-affiliate/.

Patrick Marley, "Scott Walker Says He Would Sign Ban on
Abortions after 20 Weeks." *Milwaukee Wisconsin Journal
Sentinel*, March 3, 2015. http://archive.jsonline.com/news/
statepolitics/walker-he-will-sign-abortion-ban-after-20-years
-b99455459z1-294898821.html/.

John Kasich, On the Issues: https://www.ontheissues.org/
Governor/John_Kasich_Abortion.htm.

https://www.sba-list.org/newsroom/press-releases/susan-b
-anthony-list-questions-gov-kasichs-roe-v-wade-statement.

https://www.govtrack.us/congress/bills/108/s3.

Brett LoGiurato, *Business Insider*, September 16, 2015. https://
www.businessinsider.com/carly-fiorina-planned-parenthood
-debate-2015-9.

David Brody, "Just In: Brody File Exclusive: Donald Trump
Comes Out in Support of 20 Week Abortion Ban." *CBN
News/The Brody File*, July 22, 2015. https://www1.cbn.com/
thebrodyfile/archive/2015/07/22/just-in-brody-file-exclusive
-donald-trump-comes-out-in.

Donald Trump interview, *Fox News Sunday*, October 18, 2015.
https://www.foxnews.com/transcript/donald-trump-talks

-taxes-trade-9-11-and-why-he-takes-personal-shots-at
-political-rivals.

Steven Ertelt, "Leading Pro-life Women Tell Pro-life Voters: Don't Vote for Donald Trump, Can't Trust Him on Abortion." LifeNews.com, January 26, 2016. https://www.lifenews.com/2016/01/26/leading-pro-life-women-tell-pro-life-voters-dont-vote-for-donald-trump-cant-trust-him-on-abortion.

Robert Costa and Jenna Johnson, "Evangelical Leader Jerry Falwell Jr. Endorses Trump." *Washington Post*, January 26, 2016. https://www.washingtonpost.com/news/post-politics/wp/2016/01/26/evangelical-leader-jerry-falwell-jr-endorses-trump/.

Donald Trump, "My Vision for a Culture of Life." *Washington Examiner*, January 23, 2016. https://www.washingtonexaminer.com/donald-trump-op-ed-my-vision-for-a-culture-of-life.

https://www.c-span.org/video/?c4624156/prioritize-important-aspect-choosing-supreme-court-justice&start=4993.

MSNBC town hall, March 30, 2016. https://www.cnbc.com/video/2016/03/30/trump-some-form-of-punishment-needed-for-abortion.html.

David Weigel, *Washington Post Daily 202*, July 21, 2016. https://www.washingtonpost.com/news/powerpost/paloma/daily-202/2016/07/21/daily-202-cruz-s-convention-gambit-backfiring-badly-and-now-he-s-on-the-defensive/578fcbf9cd96926bdf5624cd/.

Jamie Dean, "Ted Talks." *World*, July 21, 2016. https://world.wng.org/2016/07/ted_talks.

Ian Schwartz, "View Co-host to Clinton: Are You Saying a Child, Just Hours before Delivery, Has No Constitutional Rights?; Hillary: Yes." RealClearPolitics, April 5, 2016. https://www.realclearpolitics.com/video/2016/04/05/view_co-host_to_clinton_are_you_saying_a_child_just_hours_before_delivery_has_no_constitutional_rights_hillary_yes.html.

Morning Edition, October 12, 2016. https://www.npr.org/2016/
    10/12/497637779/conservative-female-voters-disagreeon
    -trump-tape-fallout.
https://www.c-span.org/video/?414228-1/presidential-nominees
    -debate-university-nevada-las-vegas.
SBA List 2016 Election Report: https://www.sba-list.org/2016
    -election-report.
Joel Gehrke, "Hillary Clinton: 'Religious Beliefs Have to Be
    Changed' to Accommodate Abortion." *National Review*,
    April 24, 2015. https://www.nationalreview.com/2015/
    04/hillary-clinton-religious-beliefs-have-be-changed
    -accommodate-abortion-joel-gehrke/.
Katie Reilly, "Read Hillary Clinton's 'Basket of Deplorables'
    Remarks about Donald Trump Supporters." *Time*,
    September 10, 2016. https://time.com/4486502/hillary
    -clinton-basket-of-deplorables-transcript/.

Chapter 3

"American Honey," Cary Ryan Barlowe, Hillary Lee Lindsey, and
    Shane Stevens, © Major Bob Music Inc.
The original court decision from Judge Larkins in *Teel vs. Pitt Board
    of Education* was handed down in 1967 (https://casetext.com/
    case/teel-v-pitt-county-board-of-education); a later decision in
    1970 imposed busing as a remedy. https://www.clearinghouse
    .net/chDocs/public/SD-NC-0005-0001.pdf.
C. S. Lewis, *Mere Christianity* (Macmillan, 1952).
U.S. Department of Justice, U.S. Attorney's Office, District of
    Columbia, "District Man Sentenced to 46 Months in Prison
    for Possession of Child Pornography," July 15, 2015. https://
    www.justice.gov/usao-dc/pr/district-man-sentenced-46
    -months-prison-possession-child-pornography.
Pope John Paul II, *Familiaris Consortio*. http://w2.vatican.va/
    content/john-paul-ii/en/apost_exhortations/documents/
    hf_jp-ii_exh_19811122_familiaris-consortio.html.

Pope John Paul II, *Address of His Holiness John Paul II to the 34th General Assembly of the United Nations* (New York: Vatican Publishing House, 1979). https://w2.vatican.va/content/john-paul-ii/en/speeches/1979/october/documents/hf_jp-ii_spe_19791002_general-assembly-onu.html.

Chapter 4

Michael Tackett, "Long Battle Returned Abortion to High Court." *Chicago Tribune*, January 15, 1989. https://www.chicagotribune.com/news/ct-xpm-1989-01-15-8902250670-story.html.

Dan Balz and Ruth Marcus, "In Year since Webster, Abortion Debate Defies Predictions." *Washington Post*, July 3, 1990. https://www.washingtonpost.com/archive/politics/1990/07/03/in-year-since-webster-abortiondebate-defies-predictions/b30df2ea-8ea8-4a3f-b29f-1f740df63760/.

Vote to amend H.R. 2990, Labor, Health, and Human Services Appropriations, to concur with certain Senate Amendments, October 11, 1989. https://www.govtrack.us/congress/votes/101-1989/h267.

W. James Antle III, "McGovern's Pro-life Paradox." *American Conservative*, October 22, 2012. https://www.theamericanconservative.com/articles/george-mcgoverns-pro-life-paradox/.

Republican Party Platform of 1972 Online by Gerhard Peters and John T. Woolley, American Presidency Project. https://www.presidency.ucsb.edu/node/273411.

1976 Democratic Party Platform Online by Gerhard Peters and John T. Woolley, American Presidency Project. https://www.presidency.ucsb.edu/node/273251.

Republican Party Platform of 1976 Online by Gerhard Peters and John T. Woolley, American Presidency Project. https://www.presidency.ucsb.edu/node/273415.

"Jimmy Carter on Abortion: U.S. President 1977–1981." On the
    Issues. https://www.ontheissues.org/celeb/Jimmy_Carter
    _Abortion.htm.
"Gerald Ford on Abortion: U.S. President 1974–1977." On the
    Issues. https://www.ontheissues.org/Celeb/Gerald_Ford
    _Abortion.htm.
John Nichols, "Betty Ford: Feminist, Social Liberal, Republican."
    Nation, July 9, 2011. https://www.thenation.com/article/
    archive/betty-ford-feminist-social-liberal-republican/.
"Abortion History Timeline." National Right to Life Committee.
    http://www.nrlc.org/abortion/history/.
Ramesh Ponnuru, *The Party of Death* (Washington, DC: Regnery,
    2006), p. 24, 25.
Ben Smith, "Abortion Flips, the Listicle." Politico, April 8,
    2011. https://www.politico.com/blogs/ben-smith/2011/04/
    abortion-flips-the-listicle-034858.
Bush veto message: https://www.senate.gov/legislative/vetoes/
    messages/BushGHW/HR2990-Hdoc-101-102.pdf.
Associated Press, "House Falls 51 Votes Short of Upsetting
    Abortion Veto: No Medicaid for Victims of Rape, Incest." *Los
    Angeles Times*, October 25, 1989. https://www.latimes.com/
    archives/la-xpm-1989-10-25-mn-729-story.html.
Vote totals: https://www.govtrack.us/congress/votes/101-1989/
    h295.
https://www.c-span.org/video/?c4740051/mobilize-womens
    -lives-rally-1989.
National Right to Life Committee, "Presidential Record on Life."
    http://www.nrlc.org/uploads/records/bush41record0608
    .pdf.
Anthony Depalma, "In Campaign, Courter Aims to Pin down
    His Identity." *New York Times*, September 25, 1989. https://
    www.nytimes.com/1989/09/25/nyregion/in-campaign
    -courter-aims-to-pin-down-his-identity.html.

Chapter 5

Clarence Thomas Confirmation Hearing, October 11, 1991.
    https://www.c-span.org/video/?22099-1/thomas-hearing-day
    -1-part-4.
Felicity Barringer, "The 1992 Campaign: Campaign Issues;
    Clinton and Gore Shifted on Abortion." *New York Times*,
    July 20, 1992. https://www.nytimes.com/1992/07/20/us/the
    -1992-campaign-campaign-issues-clinton-and-gore-shifted
    -on-abortion.html.
"Setting Priorities for 'Emily's List.'" *Los Angeles Times*,
    October 9, 1991. https://www.latimes.com/archives/la-xpm
    -1991-10-09-vw-158-story.html.
Governors: https://www.cawp.rutgers.edu/history-women
    -governors.
Colman McCarthy, "No Choice for Antiabortion Democrats."
    Washington Post, February 11, 1992. http://groups.csail.mit
    .edu/mac/users/rauch/nvp/politics/mccarthy_democrats
    .html.
Tim Reeves, "Casey Seeks National Audience for Prodding Party
    on Abortion." *Morning Call*, April 10, 1992. https://www
    .mcall.com/news/mc-xpm-1992-04-10-2862796-story.html.
Mario Cuomo, "Religious Belief and Public Morality: A Catholic
    Governor's Perspective." September 13, 1984. http://archives
    .nd.edu/research/texts/cuomo.htm.
Planned Parenthood of Southeastern Pennsylvania v. Casey. https://
    www.law.cornell.edu/supremecourt/text/505/833.
Supreme Court justices: https://www.supremecourt.gov/about/
    members.aspx.
Rehnquist and White dissented: https://www.landmarkcases
    .org/roe-v-wade/roe-v-wade-summary-of-the-decision.
Gallup, "Abortion." January 16–18, 1992. https://news.gallup
    .com/poll/1576/abortion.aspx.
Nina Martin, "The Supreme Court Decision That Made a Mess
    of Abortion Rights." *Mother Jones*, February 29, 2016. https://

www.motherjones.com/politics/2016/02/supreme-court
-decision-mess-abortion-rights/.

Marc Morano, "Conservatives Fear Souter Repeat in Supreme
Court Choice." CNS News, July 7, 2008. https://www.cnsnews
.com/news/article/conservatives-fear-souter-repeat-supreme
-court-choice.

"The 1992 Campaign: On the Trail; Poll Gives Perot a Clear
Lead." *New York Times*, June 11, 1992. https://www.nytimes
.com/1992/06/11/us/the-1992-campaign-on-the-trail-poll
-gives-perot-a-clear-lead.html.

Reprinted in Robert Casey, *Fighting for Life* (Word Publishing,
1996).

https://history.house.gov/Exhibitions-and-Publications/
WIC/Historical-Essays/Assembling-Amplifying-Ascending/
Women-Decade/.

National Women's Coalition for Life Statement of
Commitment, April 3, 1992. https://www.priestsforlife.org/
library/2750-national-womens-coalition-for-life-statement-of
-commitment.

From the July 8, 1869, *Revolution* article "Marriage and Maternity"
(signed by "A"), p. 4.

Chapter 6

1992 Democratic Party Platform Online by Gerhard Peters and
John T. Woolley, American Presidency Project. https://www
.presidency.ucsb.edu/documents/1992-democratic-party
-platform.

Robin Toner, "Settling In: Easing Abortion Policy; Clinton
Orders Reversal of Abortion Restrictions Left By Reagan and
Bush." *New York Times*, January 23, 1993.

From the July 8, 1869, *Revolution* article "Marriage and
Maternity" (signed by "A"), p. 4.

From the *West Virginia Evening Standard*, November 17, 1875,
pp. 470–71.

From *Revolution* 4, no. 9 (September 2, 1869): pp. 138–39.

Vivian Gornick, "Good Feminist." *Boston Review*, December 8, 2014. http://bostonreview.net/books-ideas/vivian-gornick-good-feminist-solnit-rhode-cobble-gordon-henry.

Nicholas Eberstadt, "Has the 'Global War against Baby Girls' Come to America?" Institute for Family Studies, January 27, 2020. https://ifstudies.org/blog/has-the-global-war-against-baby-girls-come-to-america.

Quoted in Sue Ellen Browder, *Subverted: How I Helped the Sexual Revolution Hijack the Women's Movement* (San Francisco: Ignatius, 2015), p. 54 and chap. 5.

Rick Wartzman, "Power of the Purse: Women Are Becoming Big Spenders in Politics and on Social Causes." *Wall Street Journal*, October 17, 1994.

Joseph Esposito, "Efforts to Elect Pro-life Women Are Paying Off." *National Catholic Register*, November 22, 1998. https://www.ncregister.com/site/article/efforts_to_elect_pro_life_women_are_paying_off1.

Chapter 7

The seven SBA-endorsed woman cosponsors were Rep. Barbara Vucanovich (R-NV, 2), Rep. Linda Smith (R-WA, 3), Rep. Andrea Seastrand (R-CA, 22), Rep. Helen Chenoweth-Hage (R-ID, 1), Rep. Barbara Cubin (R-WY, at large), Rep. Ileana Ros-Lehtinen (R-FL, 18), and Rep. Enid Waldholtz (R-UT, 2).

Veto of H.R. 1833, April 10, 1996. https://www.govinfo.gov/content/pkg/CDOC-104hdoc198/pdf/CDOC-104hdoc198.pdf.

"An Unusual Medical Consensus: Partial-Birth Abortion Is Never Medically Necessary." United States Conference of Catholic Bishops (USCCB) Secretariat for Pro-life Activities, May 27, 1997. http://www.usccb.org/issues-and-action/human-life-and-dignity/abortion/an-unusual-medical-consensus-partial-birth-abortion-is-never-necessary.cfm.

Ronald Brownstein and John Broder, "Clinton Clashes with Dole over Abortion Stance." *Los Angeles Times*, May 24, 1996.

Elizabeth Kolbert, "Abortion, Dole's Sword in '74, Returns to Confront Him in '96." *New York Times*, July 8, 1996.

1996 Republican Party platform: https://www.presidency.ucsb .edu/documents/republican-party-platform-1996.

Byron P. White, "Dole Speaks on Taboo Topic, Criticizes Clinton on 'Partial-Birth Abortion.'" *Chicago Tribune*, September 8, 1996. https://www.chicagotribune.com/news/ct-xpm-1996 -09-08-9609080260-story,amp.html.

https://www.govtrack.us/congress/votes/104-1996/s301.

Celinda Lake memo: http://www.nrlc.org/archive/abortion/ pba/LakememoPBA.pdf.

Mary McGrory, "Kemp Gets Gored." *Washington Post*, October 13, 1996. https://www.washingtonpost.com/archive/opinions/ 1996/10/13/kemp-gets-gored/ed229b0e-bb1a-4e0c-adc4 -aea8a05c74a2/.

Mary McGrory, "Catholics Relent, Stick with Clinton." *St. Louis Post-Dispatch*, November 3, 1996. https://www.questia.com/ newspaper/1P2-33038727/catholics-relent-stick-with-clinton.

Charles E. Cook, "Political Surveyor." *Roll Call*, February 27, 1997, p. 8.

https://www.govtrack.us/congress/votes/105-1998/s277.

University of Wisconsin / Wisconsin State Journal Poll, August 7–26, 1998.

https://www.nytimes.com/1998/10/15/us/political-briefing -senate-race-turns-nasty-in-wisconsin.html.

Bruce Morton, "Feingold Faces Tough Re-election Fight in Wisconsin." CNN, October 22, 1998. https://edition.cnn.com/ ALLPOLITICS/stories/1998/10/22/wisconsin.senate/.

Bush promise: https://www.ontheissues.org/celeb/george_w_ _bush_abortion.htm.

Stenberg v. Carhart: https://www.law.cornell.edu/supct/html/99 -830.ZS.html.

https://news.gallup.com/poll/2953/abortion-major-issue
-critical-presidential-vote-most-americans.aspx.
https://debates.org/voter-education/debate-transcripts/october
-3-2000-transcript/.
https://www.pollingreport.com/2000.htm.

Chapter 8

This NRLC fact sheet reports the 80 percent-plus number:
https://www.nrlc.org/archive/Federal/CCPA/why_we_need
_CCPA.htm.
Gallup polling reflects a slightly lower number on parental
notification overall but does not ask specifically about
crossing state lines: https://news.gallup.com/poll/20203/
americans-favor-parental-involvement-teen-abortion
-decisions.aspx.
Michael Dobbs, "Obama's Voting Record on Abortion."
Washington Post, February 6, 2008. http://voices
.washingtonpost.com/fact-checker/2008/02/obamas_voting
_record_on_aborti_1.html.
Steven Ertelt, "Barack Obama Would Back Daughters'
Abortion, 'Don't Punish Them with a Baby.'" LifeNews.com,
March 31, 2008. https://www.lifenews.com/2008/03/31/nat
-3827/.
Jake Tapper, "Pro-life or Just Anti-McCain?" *Salon*, January 14,
2000. https://www.salon.com/2000/01/14/mccain_66/.
Kathryn Jean Lopez, "Susan B. Anthony List Is Happy." *National
Review*, August 29, 2008. https://www.nationalreview.com/
corner/susan-b-anthony-list-happy-kathryn-jean-lopez/
amp/.
Igor Volsky, "Christie Todd Whitman Cautions Republicans
against Overreaching, Says Palin Lacks 'Depth.'"
ThinkProgress, December 12, 2010. https://thinkprogress
.org/christie-todd-whitman-cautions-republicans-against
-overreaching-says-palin-lacks-depth-607c4e4527f3/.

"Cindy McCain on Abortion, Creationism." CBS News, September 3, 2008. https://www.cbsnews.com/news/cindy -mccain-on-abortion-creationism/.

Jonathan Martin, "Cindy McCain Opposes Abortion but Would Not Support Overturning Roe." Politico, September 3, 2008. https://www.politico.com/blogs/jonathanmartin/0908/ Cindy_McCain_opposes_abortion_but_would_not_support _overturning_Roe.html.

Tony Lee, "Former McCain Adviser Nicolle Wallace Trashes Sarah Palin on 'The View.'" Breitbart, March 14, 2014. https://www .breitbart.com/the-media/2014/03/14/nicolle-wallace-trashes -palin-praises-christie-bill-clinton-jeb-bush-on-the-view/.

Dan Amira, "Michele Bachmann Has the Spirit of a Psychotic Clown Serial Killer." *New York Magazine*, June 27, 2011. http://nymag.com/intelligencer/2011/06/michele _bachmann_says_she_has.html.

Obama's "fifty-seven states" gaffe: https://www.reuters.com/ video/watch/idWAO1209788800644.

"Ad Depicts Candidate Robbing Corpse, Soldier." Fox News, September 28, 2004. https://www.foxnews.com/story/ad -depicts-candidate-robbing-corpse-soldier.

Kerry Eleveld, "The Gay Goodfellas." *Advocate*, June 21, 2008. https://www.advocate.com/news/2008/06/21/gay-goodfellas.

Jason Kosena, "Attack Ads Begin against Musgrave." *Colorado Independent*, June 24, 2008. https://www .coloradoindependent.com/2008/06/24/attack-ads-begin -against-musgrave/.

Chapter 9

John McCormack, "Scozzafava Calls the Cops." *Weekly Standard*, October 19, 2009. https://www.washingtonexaminer.com/ weekly-standard/scozzafava-calls-the-cops.

House Republican women, 111th U.S. Congress (2009–11): https://history.house.gov/Exhibitions-and-Publications/

WIC/Historical-Data/Women-Representatives-and-Senators
-by-Congress/.

"Republican Scozzafava Endorses Democrat after Exiting N.Y.
Congressional Race." Fox News, November 1, 2009. https://
www.foxnews.com/politics/republican-scozzafava-endorses
-democrat-after-exiting-n-y-congressional-race.

Jeremy W. Peters, "Right Battles G.O.P. in a Pivotal Race in
New York." *New York Times*, October 26, 2009. https://www
.nytimes.com/2009/10/27/nyregion/27upstate.html.

Marjorie Dannenfelser, "If Republicans Keep Ignoring
Abortion, They'll Lose in the Midterm Elections."
Washington Post, March 14, 2010. https://www
.washingtonpost.com/wp-dyn/content/article/2010/03/12/
AR2010031201793.html.

Chapter 10

Irvin Molotsky, "Former Gov. Robert P. Casey Dies at 68;
Pennsylvania Democrat Opposed Abortion." *New York Times*,
May 31, 2000. https://www.nytimes.com/2000/05/31/us/
former-gov-robert-p-casey-dies-at-68-pennsylvania-democrat
-opposed-abortion.html.

"Congressional Record—House." November 7, 2009. https://
www.govinfo.gov/content/pkg/CREC-2009-11-07/pdf/CREC
-2009-11-07-pt1-PgH12623-3.pdf#page=299.

"Obama Health Care Speech to Congress." September 9, 2009.
https://www.nytimes.com/2009/09/10/us/politics/10obama
.text.html.

U.S. Government Accountability Office report, September 15,
2014. http://images.politico.com/global/2014/09/15/
embargoed_gao_report.html.

"ObamacareAbortion.com 2020 Fact Sheet." Family Research
Council. https://downloads.frc.org/EF/EF19L03.pdf.

Shailagh Murray and Lori Montgomery, "House Passes Health-
Care Reform Bill without Republican Votes." *Washington Post*,

March 22, 2010. https://www.washingtonpost.com/wp-dyn/
content/article/2010/03/21/AR2010032100943_2.html?sid=
ST2010032201830.

"Breaking—Stupak a Yes." Politico, March 21, 2010. https://
www.politico.com/livepulse/0310/BREAKING__Stupak_a
_yes.html.

https://www.govtrack.us/congress/votes/111-2010/h165.

Sean J. Miller, "Anti-abortion Group: Democrat Deserves
'Medal' for 'No' Vote." *Hill*, March 15, 2010. https://thehill
.com/blogs/ballot-box/house-races/86927-anti-abortion
-group-driehaus-deserves-medal-for-no-vote-.

"Standing—Preenforcement Challenges—*Susan B. Anthony List v.
Driehaus.*" *Harvard Law Review*. https://harvardlawreview
.org/wp-content/uploads/2014/11/SBA_list_v_driehaus
.pdf.

"*Susan B. Anthony List v. Driehaus*—Amicus Brief." American Civil
Liberties Union. https://www.aclu.org/legal-document/susan
-b-anthony-list-v-driehaus-amicus-brief.

"Kathy Dahlkemper for Life" ad: http://www.youtube.com/
watch?v=8BBkZAVFsLA.

"Bishops Call for Vigilance in Implementing, Correcting Health
Care Law." *Long Island Catholic*, March 24, 2010. https://
www.newspaper.licatholic.org/news/bishops-call-vigilance
-implementing-correcting-health-care-law.

Jill Stanek, "Democrats for Life Betrays Pro-life Movement."
World Net Daily, November 17, 2010. https://www.wnd.com/
2010/11/229201/.

Ayotte v. Planned Parenthood of Northern New England. https://
www.oyez.org/cases/2005/04-1144?_escaped_fragment_=.

Jill Stanek, "Judge Assigned to Pro-life Group Lawsuit Is Obama
Appointee and Former Cincy Planned Parenthood Prez."
October 20, 2010. http://www.jillstanek.com/2010/10/judge
-assigned-to-pro-life-group-lawsuit-is-obama-appointee-and
-former-cincy-planned-parenthood-prez/.

Susan B. Anthony List, et al. v. Ohio Elections Commission (Amicus).
    ACLU of Ohio. https://www.acluohio.org/archives/cases/
    susan-b-anthony-list.
Susan B. Anthony List v. Driehaus, 573 U.S. 149 (2014). https://
    supreme.justia.com/cases/federal/us/573/149/#tab-opinion
    -1970937.
Laura Bassett, "Supreme Court Moves toward Legalizing Lying
    in Campaigns." Huffington Post, June 16, 2014. https://www
    .huffpost.com/entry/scotus-sba-list_n_5499404.
List v. Ohio Elections Comm'n, 45 F. Supp. 3d 765 (S.D. Ohio
    2014). https://casetext.com/case/list-v-ohio-elections
    -commn-1.

Chapter 11

Calvin Woodward, "Republicans Promise an Era of Limited
    Government." *Savannah Morning News*, November 3, 2010.
    https://www.savannahnow.com/article/20101103/NEWS/
    311039775?template=ampart.
https://www.congress.gov/bill/112th-congress/house-bill/3.
Publius, "House Votes to Repeal Obamacare." Breitbart,
    January 19, 2011. https://www.breitbart.com/politics/2011/
    01/19/house-votes-to-repeal-obamacare/.
Andrew Ferguson, "Ride along with Mitch." *Weekly Standard*,
    June 14, 2010. https://www.washingtonexaminer.com/weekly
    -standard/ride-along-with-mitch.
John McCormack, "More on Mitch Daniels' 'Truce.'" *Weekly
    Standard*, June 8, 2010. https://www.washingtonexaminer
    .com/weekly-standard/more-on-mitch-daniels-truce.
Frank Cannon, "How to Lose the Presidential Nomination in
    Two Days." Fox News, June 18, 2010. https://www.foxnews
    .com/opinion/how-to-lose-the-presidential-nomination-in
    -two-days.
Jon Ward, "Barbour Warns Republicans Not to Go down 'Rabbit
    Trails.'" Daily Caller, September 8, 2010.

https://dailycaller.com/2010/09/08/barbour-warns
-republicans-not-to-go-down-rabbit-trails.

Ben Smith, "Steele: Abortion an 'Individual Choice.'" Politico,
March 11, 2009. https://www.politico.com/blogs/ben-smith/
2009/03/steele-abortion-an-individual-choice-016721.

Marjorie Dannenfelser, "The Truce That Really Counts."
National Review, January 11, 2011. https://www
.nationalreview.com/2011/01/truce-really-counts-marjorie
-dannenfelser/.

Dana Milbank, "There's No Argument Here." *Philadelphia
Inquirer*, January 5, 2011. https://www.inquirer.com/philly/
opinion/inquirer/20110105_There_s_no_argument_here
.html.

The Daily Show with Jon Stewart, "Top of the GOPs." January 4,
2011. http://www.cc.com/video-clips/4xehei/the-daily-show
-with-jon-stewart-top-of-the-gops.

David Lightman, "Romney's Flip-Flop on Abortion Dogs His
Campaign." McClatchy, October 25, 2007. https://www
.mcclatchydc.com/news/politics-government/article24471109
.html.

Ta-Nehisi Coates, "Recalling a Pro-choice Mitt Romney." *Atlantic*,
February 22, 2012. https://www.theatlantic.com/politics/
archive/2012/02/recalling-a-pro-choice-mitt-romney/
253452/.

Louis Jacobson, "Mitt Romney Evolved Significantly in His
Position on Abortion." PolitiFact, May 15, 2012. https://www
.politifact.com/factchecks/2012/may/15/mitt-romney/mitt
-romney-evolved-significantly-his-position-abo/.

"Induced Abortion in the United States." Alan Guttmacher
Institute, September 2019. https://www.guttmacher.org/fact
-sheet/induced-abortion-united-states.

Jon Ward, "Mitt Romney Refuses to Sign Pro-life Pledge."
Huffington Post, June 17, 2011. https://www.huffpost.com/
entry/mitt-romney-pro-life_n_879582.

Jennifer Rubin, "An Abortion Pledge Mess." *Washington Post*,
   June 18, 2011. https://www.washingtonpost.com/blogs/right
   -turn/post/an-abortion-pledge-mess/2011/03/29/AGesgYaH
   _blog.html.

Mitt Romney, "My Pro-life Pledge." *National Review*, June 18,
   2011. https://www.nationalreview.com/corner/my-pro-life
   -pledge-mitt-romney/.

Michael D. Shear and Jim Rutenberg, "Santorum Suspends
   Presidential Campaign." *New York Times*, April 10, 2010.
   https://thecaucus.blogs.nytimes.com/2012/04/10/santorum
   -to-suspend-presidential-campaign/.

Charles Mahtesian, "Who Matters to Democrats." Politico,
   September 4, 2012. https://www.politico.com/story/2012/09/
   read-their-lips-who-matters-to-democrats-080664.

John Eligon and Michael Schwirtz, "Senate Candidate Provokes
   Ire with 'Legitimate Rape' Comment." *New York Times*,
   August 19, 2012. https://www.nytimes.com/2012/08/20/
   us/politics/todd-akin-provokes-ire-with-legitimate-rape
   -comment.html.

"George Romney's 'Brainwashing'—1967." *Washington Post*.
   https://www.washingtonpost.com/wp-srv/politics/special/
   clinton/frenzy/romney.htm.

Lucy Madison, "Richard Mourdock: Even Pregnancy from Rape
   Something 'God Intended.'" CBS News, October 24, 2012.
   https://www.cbsnews.com/news/richard-mourdock-even
   -pregnancy-from-rape-something-god-intended/.

Seung Min Kim, "Donnelly Upsets Mourdock in Indiana."
   Politico, November 6, 2012. https://www.politico.com/story/
   2012/11/donnelly-upsets-mourdock-in-indiana-083440.

Lori Robertson, "Planned Parenthood and Mammograms."
   Factcheck.org, October 18, 2012. https://www.factcheck.org/
   2012/10/planned-parenthood-and-mammograms/.

Leigh Ann Caldwell, "Obama Campaign Ad Hits Romney on
   Abortion." CBS News, October 25, 2012. https://www.cbsnews
   .com/news/obama-campaign-ad-hits-romney-on-abortion/.

Jeremy W. Peters, "Romney Clarifies Abortion Stance." *New York Times*, October 17, 2012. https://www.nytimes.com/2012/10/18/us/politics/romney-clarifies-abortion-stance.html.

Stephen P. White, "An Abortion Survivor Wants to Know . . ." *National Review*, August 29, 2012. https://www.nationalreview.com/corner/abortion-survivor-wants-know-stephen-p-white/.

Chapter 12

Austin Ruse, "Romney's Abandonment of Social Issues Contributed to His Defeat." *Crisis Magazine*, November 9, 2012. https://www.crisismagazine.com/2012/romneys-abandonment-of-social-issues-contributed-to-his-defeat.

Thomas B. Edsall, "The Republican Autopsy Report." *New York Times*, March 20, 2013. https://opinionator.blogs.nytimes.com/2013/03/20/the-republican-autopsy-report/.

Garance Franke-Ruta, "What You Need to Read in the RNC Election-Autopsy Report." *Atlantic*, March 18, 2013. https://www.theatlantic.com/politics/archive/2013/03/what-you-need-to-read-in-the-rnc-election-autopsy-report/274112/.

Gallup, "'Pro-choice' Americans at Record-Low 41%." May 23, 2012. https://news.gallup.com/poll/154838/pro-choice-americans-record-low.aspx.

https://news.gallup.com/poll/1576/abortion.aspx.

https://news.gallup.com/poll/246206/abortion-trends-age.aspx.

https://www.sba-list.org/wp-content/uploads/2017/08/Public-Polling-on-ProLife-Hispanics.pdf.

Frank Cannon, Maggie Gallagher, and Rich Danker, "Building a Winning GOP Coalition: The Lessons of 2012." https://americanprinciplesproject.org/wp-content/uploads/2018/09/BuildingAWinningGOPCoalition.pdf.

https://www.congress.gov/bill/113th-congress/house-bill/1797/text/rh.

"Fact Check: Do Only 7 Countries Allow Elective Abortions after 20 Weeks of Pregnancy?" *Washington Post*, October 6,

2017. https://www.washingtonpost.com/video/politics/fact
-check-do-only-7-countries-allow-elective-abortions-after-20
-weeks-of-pregnancy/2017/10/09/23815202-aacd-11e7-9a98
-07140d2eed02_video.html.

https://news.gallup.com/poll/160058/majority-americans
-support-roe-wade-decision.aspx.

Steven Ertelt, "Majority of Americans Back 20-Week Abortion
Ban, Women More Than Men." LifeNews.com, August 2,
2013. https://www.lifenews.com/2013/08/02/majority-of
-americans-back-20-week-abortion-ban-women-more-than
-men/.

Jake Miller, "Poll: Majority of Americans Support 20-Week
Abortion Ban." CBS News, July 25, 2013. https://www
.cbsnews.com/news/poll-majority-of-americans-support-20
-week-abortion-ban/.

https://www.congress.gov/bill/113th-congress/house-bill/1797.

Beth Reinhard, "Emily's List Candidates Are Quiet on
Abortion." *Wall Street Journal*, July 13, 2014. https://www.wsj
.com/articles/emilys-list-candidates-are-quiet-on-abortion
-1405303567.

"Joni Ernst Wins Election, First Woman to Represent Iowa in
US Senate." WHOtv.com / Channel 13 News, Des Moines, IA,
November 4, 2014. https://whotv.com/2014/11/04/joni-ernst
-wins-election-first-woman-to-represent-iowa-in-us-senate/.

Lauren French and Jake Sherman, "GOP Women Object to Rape
Clause in 20-Week Abortion Bill." Politico, January 16, 2015.
https://www.politico.com/story/2015/01/abortion-bill-rape
-victims-114324.

Jill Stanek, "Is Rep. Renee Ellmers a Pro-choice Mole?" jillstanek
.com, January 16, 2015. https://www.jillstanek.com/2015/01/
rep-renee-ellmers-prochoice-mole/.

https://heavy.com/news/2019/01/march-for-life-crowd-size
-numbers-attended/.

Austin Ruse, "Exclusive: Pro-life Leaders Call for Ellmers' Ouster from Congress." Breitbart, January 22, 2015. https://www .breitbart.com/politics/2015/01/22/exclusive-pro-life-leaders -call-for-ellmers-ouster-from-congress/.

https://www.congress.gov/bill/114th-congress/house-bill/ 36/all-actions?overview=closed&q={%22roll-call-vote%22: %22all%22}&KWICView=false.

"Holding Defeats Ellmers in Member versus Member Primary." Politico. https://www.politico.com/story/2016/06/holding -defeats-ellmers-in-member-versus-member-primary-224032 %5C.

Chapter 13

Gosnell grand jury report: https://cdn.cnsnews.com/ documents/Gosnell,%20Grand%20Jury%20Report.pdf.

Kirsten Powers, "Philadelphia Abortion Clinic Horror." *USA Today*, April 11, 2013. https://www.usatoday.com/story/ opinion/2013/04/10/philadelphia-abortion-clinic-horror -column/2072577/.

Mollie Hemingway, "*Washington Post*'s Kermit Gosnell Denialism Is Out of Control." Federalist, June 27, 2016. https://thefederalist.com/2016/06/27/washington-posts -kermit-gosnell-denialism-is-out-of-control/.

Brief for Concerned Women of America and Susan B. Anthony List as *amicus curiae* in support of respondents. *Whole Woman's Health v. Hellerstedt*, 136 S.Ct. 2292 (2016). https:// s27319.pcdn.co/wp-content/uploads/2016/02/02.16-SBA -CWA-Whoel-Womens-Health.pdf.

https://www.sba-list.org/newsroom/press-releases/scotus-raises -2016-stakes-pro-lifers.

Ruth Bader Ginsburg's opinion in *Whole Woman's Health v. Hellerstedt*: https://www.supremecourt.gov/opinions/15pdf/ 15-274_new_e18f.pdf.

http://www.centerformedicalprogress.org/cmp/investigative
    -footage/.

"Annual Report, 2018–2019." Planned Parenthood. https://
    www.plannedparenthood.org/uploads/filer_public/2e/da/
    2eda3f50-82aa-4ddb-acce-c2854c4ea80b/2018-2019_annual
    _report.pdf.

https://www.govtrack.us/congress/votes/114-2015/h505.

Sarah Ferris, "House Creates Panel to Investigate Planned
    Parenthood." *Hill*, October 7, 2015. https://thehill.com/
    policy/healthcare/256254-house-creates-panel-to-investigate
    -planned-parenthood.

"Carly Fiorina Rips Planned Parenthood." CNN, September 16,
    2015. https://www.youtube.com/watch?v=2p_CyDI87Rc&
    feature=emb_title.

Summary of Select Panel findings: https://www
    .nationalrighttolifenews.org/2017/02/select-congressional
    -panel-releases-report-on-planned-parenthood-and-fetal
    -tissue-part-one/.

Public writings and speeches of Margaret Sanger, collected by
    NYU: https://www.nyu.edu/projects/sanger/webedition/app/
    documents/show.php?sangerDoc=306641.xml.

"'What Kind of Society Do You Want to Live In?': Inside the
    Country Where Down Syndrome Is Disappearing." CBS
    News, August 14, 2017. https://www.cbsnews.com/news/
    down-syndrome-iceland/.

"Abortion Surveillance—United States, 2016." U.S. Centers
    for Disease Control and Prevention. https://www.cdc.gov/
    mmwr/volumes/68/ss/ss6811a1.htm.

"Women of Color in the United States: Quick Take." Catalyst
    Research, March 19, 2020. https://www.catalyst.org/research/
    women-of-color-in-the-united-states/.

Dr. Michael New, "Guttmacher Report Shows Pro-life Progress
    Continues as U.S. Abortion Rates Decline." Charlotte Lozier
    Institute, September 18, 2019. https://lozierinstitute.org/

guttmacher-report-shows-pro-life-progress-continues-as-u-s
-abortion-rates-decline/.

Tessa Longbons, "Abortion Reporting: New York City (2017)."
Charlotte Lozier Institute, November 1, 2019. https://
lozierinstitute.org/abortion-reporting-new-york-city-2017/.

Tessa Longbons, "Abortion Reporting: New York City (2016)."
Charlotte Lozier Institute, December 19, 2018. https://
lozierinstitute.org/abortion-reporting-new-york-city-2016/.

"Planned Parenthood: 'Irreplaceable' and 'Life-Saving'?"
CLI, August 2, 2017. https://lozierinstitute.org/planned
-parenthood-irreplaceable-and-lifesaving/.

https://cnsnews.com/commentary/michael-new/planned
-parenthoods-annual-report-shows-big-abortion-needs-big
-government.

Alexandra DeSanctis, "Planned Parenthood Offers Bare
Minimum of Prenatal Care." *National Review*, January 25,
2017. https://www.nationalreview.com/corner/planned
-parenthood-prenatal-care-not-groups-focus/.

C-SPAN: https://www.c-span.org/video/?c4553077/user-clip
-cecile-richards-testifies-re-mammograms.

Sarah Kliff and Shane Goldmacher, "Why Leana Wen Quickly
Lost Support at Planned Parenthood." *New York Times*,
July 17, 2019. https://www.nytimes.com/2019/07/17/us/
politics/planned-parenthood-wen.html.

https://www.centerformedicalprogress.org/cmp/support-our
-legal-defense/.

Sam Dorman, "Judge Dismisses Some Criminal Charges in
Planned Parenthood Video Case." Fox News, December 7,
2019. https://www.foxnews.com/politics/judge-dismisses
-some-criminal-charges-daleiden.

https://www.latimes.com/opinion/editorials/la-ed-planned
-parenthood-charges-20170330-story.html.

Lianne Laurence, "StemExpress CEO Admits Selling Beating
Baby Hearts, Intact Baby Heads in Daleiden Hearing."

LifeSiteNews, September 6, 2019. https://www.lifesitenews
.com/news/stemexpress-ceo-admits-selling-beating-baby
-hearts-intact-baby-heads-in-daleiden-hearing.

Sabrina Tavernise, "Planned Parenthood Awarded $2 Million in
Lawsuit over Secret Videos." *New York Times*, November 15,
2019. https://www.nytimes.com/2019/11/15/us/planned
-parenthood-lawsuit-secret-videos.html?auth=login-email&
login=email.

Chapter 14

"House Budget Bill Repeals 'Mexico City Policy' on NGO
Abortion Funding." Catholic News Service, January 8, 2019.
https://cruxnow.com/church-in-the-usa/2019/01/house
-budget-bill-repeals-mexico-city-policy-on-ngo-abortion
-funding/.

https://www.congress.gov/bill/116th-congress/house-bill/962.

https://www.republicanwhip.gov/endinfanticide/.

Marc Thiessen, "At the March for Life, Trump Will Be Greeted
as a Pro-life Hero—Because He Is One." *Washington Post*,
January 23, 2020. https://www.washingtonpost.com/
opinions/trump-has-embraced-the-pro-life-movement-in
-a-way-no-other-president-has/2020/01/23/d4ecab5c-3e11
-11ea-b90d-5652806c3b3a_story.html#click=https://t.co/
AWb5Qeb5eH.

Jessie Hellmann, "Trump Campaign Launches 'Pro-life'
Coalition for Reelection Bid." *Hill*, January 24, 2020. https://
thehill.com/policy/healthcare/479713-trump-campaign
-launches-pro-life-coalition-to-help-reelection-bid.

Official White House transcript—"Remarks by President Trump
at the 47th Annual March for Life": https://www.whitehouse
.gov/briefings-statements/remarks-president-trump-47th
-annual-march-life/.

Transcript, "Marjorie Dannenfelser's Speech at 2020 March
for Life Rally": https://www.sba-list.org/newsroom/latest

-news/marjorie-dannenfelsers-speech-at-2020-march-for
-life-rally.

Elizabeth Dias, Annie Karni, and Sabrina Tavernise, "Trump
Tells Anti-abortion Marchers, 'Unborn Children Have Never
Had a Stronger Defender in the White House.'" *New York
Times*, January 24, 2020. https://www.nytimes.com/2020/01/
24/us/politics/trump-abortion-march-life.html.

Emily Bohatch, "2020 Presidential Hopefuls to Speak at
Planned Parenthood Abortion Forum in SC." *State*, June 12,
2019. https://www.thestate.com/news/politics-government/
election/article231469148.html#storylink=cpy.

Alexandra DeSanctis, "On Abortion, One 2020 Democrat Hit
the Gas Pedal." *National Review*, June 27, 2019. https://www
.nationalreview.com/corner/julian-castro-on-abortion-one
-2020-democrat-hit-the-gas-pedal/.

Julia Manchester, "Gillibrand Compares Limiting Abortion
Rights to Racism." *Hill*, June 11, 2019.

Valerie Richardson, "Biden Puts Moderate Brand at Risk
for 2020 with Hyde Amendment Flip-Flop." *Washington
Times*, June 8, 2019. https://www.washingtontimes.com/
news/2019/jun/8/pro-lifers-warn-bidens-flip-flop-hyde
-amendment-wi/.

https://news.gallup.com/poll/211901/abortion-attitudes-stable
-no-consensus-legality.aspx.

https://www.sba-list.org/wp-content/uploads/2020/02/
National-Pain-Capable-Born-Alive-Polling-1-pager.pdf.

Scott Powers, "Anti-abortion Group Poll Says Joe Biden's Flip
Could Cost Him in General." *Florida Politics*, June 26, 2019.
https://floridapolitics.com/archives/299835-anti-abortion
-group-poll-says-joe-bidens-flip-could-cost-him-in-general.

https://www.sba-list.org/wp-content/uploads/2017/08/Public
-Polling-on-ProLife-Democrats.pdf.

Laura Bassett, "Democratic Party Draws a Line in the Sand on
Abortion Rights." Huffington Post, April 21, 2017. https://

www.huffpost.com/entry/democrats-tom-perez-abortion
-rights_n_58fa5fade4b018a9ce5b351d.

John Jalsevac, "Catholic Nancy Pelosi: Issue of Late-Term
Abortions Is 'Sacred Ground.'" LifeSiteNews, June 13, 2013.
https://www.lifesitenews.com/news/nancy-pelosi-issue-of
-late-term-abortions-is-sacred-ground.

Tré Goins-Phillips, "Pelosi: Abortion Is 'Kind of Fading as an
Issue' in the Democratic Party." Blaze, May 3, 2017. https://
www.theblaze.com/news/2017/05/03/pelosi-abortion-is-kind
-of-fading-as-an-issue-in-the-democratic-party.

Ilyse Hogue's tweet on May 2, 2017: https://twitter.com/ilyseh/
status/859558464745611265.

Tyler Olson, "Pro-life Dem Clashes with Buttigieg at Town Hall:
'We Don't Belong.'" Fox News, January 27, 2020. https://www
.foxnews.com/politics/pro-life-dem-clashes-with-buttigieg-at
-town-hall-we-dont-belong.

Patrick Goodenough, "Sanders: 'Being Pro-choice Is an
Absolutely Essential Part of Being a Democrat.'" CNS News,
February 9, 2020. https://cnsnews.com/article/national/
patrick-goodenough/sanders-being-pro-choice-absolutely
-essential-part-being.

Karen Tumulty, "Pelosi: Democratic Candidates Should Not
Be Forced to Toe Party Line on Abortion." *Washington Post*,
May 2, 2017. https://www.washingtonpost.com/politics/
pelosi-democratic-candidates-should-not-be-forced-to-toe
-party-line-on-abortion/2017/05/02/9cbc9bc6-2f68-11e7
-9534-00e4656c22aa_story.html.

Gala speech: https://www.sba-list.org/newsroom/news/vice
-president-mike-pences-speech-2017-campaign-life-gala.

Index

Tennant, Natalie, 184
Tester, Jon, 211
Texas, 198–200, 205
Thiessen, Marc, 214
Thomas, Clarence, 72–73, 156
Thompson, Fred, 120, 137–38
Thompson, Jeri, 120, 138
Title X program, 215
Tobias, Carol, 186
Toomey, Pat, 134
Tran, Kathy, 4
Trump, Donald
  attitude toward women, 25–26,
    36–37
  candidacy of, 23–31, 32–40,
    210–11
  March for Life address, 214,
    215–18, 222
  as most pro-life president, 3–5,
    214–15, 221
  personal characteristics, 28
  on *Roe v. Wade*, 26–27
  statements on abortion, 33,
    35–36, 216–17

unborn children
  Fourteenth Amendment and,
    108
  pain felt by, 166, 181
  protection of, 24, 26, 63, 218
  rights of, 33–34, 37–38, 59, 103
U.N. Population Fund, 214
USA Today, 197–98

Valentine, Natalie, 136
Virginia, 4–5
Vucanovich, Barbara, 68

Wagner, Ann, 192, 213
Waldholtz, Enid, 96
Walker, Scott, 19–20
Wallace, Chris, 20, 25
Wallace, Nicolle, 124
Wall Street Journal, 94–95, 183
Walorski, Jackie, 189, 192
Washington, DC, 49–50, 58
Washington Examiner, 27
Washington Post, 76, 93, 110, 145,
    163, 168, 182, 198
  SBA List and, 31–32, 139–40,
    214
Waxman, Henry, 144
*Webster v. Reproductive Health
    Services*, 59–60, 62, 75
Weekly Standard, 133, 161
Weigel, David, 31
West Virginia, 61, 212–13
Whelan, Edward, 6
White, Byron, 77
White, Paula, 12
Whitman, Christine Todd, 123
*Whole Women's Health v.
    Hellerstedt*, 199–200
Wilder, Douglas, 67
Wisconsin, 19–20
WISH List. *See* Women in the
    Senate and House List
Woman in Charge, A (Bernstein), 88
Women in the Senate and
    House List (WISH List), 78,
    83, 163
Women Speak Out, 182
Woodhull, Victoria, 89

"Year of the Woman," 79, 85, 94

About the Author

Author Biography

Marjorie Dannenfelser is president of Susan B. Anthony List. Over the last three election cycles, SBA List and its super PAC, Women Speak Out, have reached more than 4.6 million voters by visiting voters at their homes to win a pro-life White House and secure a pro-life majority in the U.S. Senate. In January 2020, Dannenfelser was named national co-chair of the Pro-Life Voices for Trump coalition, a role she held during the 2016 campaign after securing four groundbreaking pro-life commitments from the nominee. Dannenfelser has been published widely including in *TIME, The Washington Post*, and *National Review* and profiled by *New York Magazine, The Telegraph, The New Yorker*, and *The Washington Post*. She serves on the board of Alliance Defending

Freedom, on Life Perspectives' Task Force, and was appointed to the Women's Suffrage Centennial Commission by Senate Leader McConnell. She was named one of *Politico* Magazine's Top 50 Influencers of 2018, *Washington Examiner's* top ten "Political Women on the Move," *Newsmax's* top 25 Most Influential Republican Women, and *Newsweek's* top ten "Leaders of the Christian Right." An alumna of Duke University, she and her husband Marty live in Arlington, Virginia, and have five children.

About Susan B. Anthony List

Susan B. Anthony List is a political powerhouse that delivered millions of pro-life votes key to Donald Trump's victory in 2016. A national network of more than 900,000 Americans, SBA List's mission is to end abortion by electing national leaders and advocating for laws that save lives, with a special calling to promote pro-life women leaders. Since its founding, SBA List has helped elect more than 118 pro-life candidates to the U.S. House of Representatives, 26 to the U.S. Senate, and 30 to state office.

To learn more and join the fight for life, visit www.sbalist.org.

facebook.com/SusanBAnthonyList/

twitter.com/SBAList

More Titles From Humanix Books You May Be Interested In:

Warren Buffett says:
"My friend, Ben Stein, has written a short book that tells you everything you need to know about investing (and in words you can understand). Follow Ben's advice and you will do far better than almost all investors (and I include pension funds, universities and the super-rich) who pay high fees to advisors."

In his entertaining and informative style that has captivated generations, beloved *New York Times* bestselling author, actor, and financial expert Ben Stein sets the record straight about capitalism in the United States — it is not the "rigged system" young people are led to believe.

Dr. Mehmet Oz says:
"*SNAP!* shows that personalities can be changed from what our genes or early childhood would have ordained. Invest the 30 days."

New York Times bestselling author Dr. Gary Small's breakthrough plan to improve your personality for a better life! As you read *SNAP!* you will gain a better understanding of who you are now, how others see you, and which aspects of yourself you'd like to change. You will acquire the tools you need to change your personality in just one month — it won't take years of psychotherapy, self-exploration, or re-hashing every single bad thing that's ever happened to you.

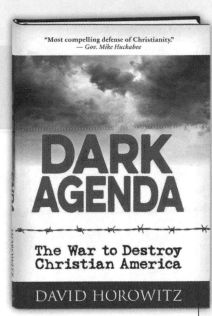